THE VOICE
OF THE OTHER

THE VOICE OF THE OTHER

Language as Illusion in the Formation of the Self

Stanley William Rothstein

PRAEGER　　　　　　　　　　Westport, Connecticut
　　　　　　　　　　　　　　　London

Library of Congress Cataloging-in-Publication Data

Rothstein, Stanley William, 1929–
  The voice of the other : language as illusion in the formation of the self / Stanley William Rothstein.
    p. cm.
  Includes bibliographical references and index.
  ISBN 0-275-94358-5 (alk. paper)
  1. Language and languages. I. Title.
  P106.R675   1993
  400—dc20   92-23059

British Library Cataloguing in Publication Data is available.

Copyright © 1993 by Stanley William Rothstein

All rights reserved. No portion of this book may be reproduced, by any process or technique, without the express written consent of the publisher.

Library of Congress Catalog Card Number: 92–23059
ISBN: 0-275-94358-5

First published in 1993

Praeger Publishers, 88 Post Road West, Westport, CT 06881
An imprint of Greenwood Publishing Group, Inc.

Printed in the United States of America

The paper used in this book complies with the Permanent Paper Standard issued by the National Information Standards Organization (Z39.48—1984).

10 9 8 7 6 5 4 3 2 1

For Susan and Stacy,
for their unconditional love and support

Contents

Preface	ix
1. The Voice of the Other: An Introduction	1
2. Language and Thought	25
3. Language and Kinship Structures	47
4. Reproduction	69
5. The Function of Language in Pedagogic Work	93
6. The Imaginary World of the Classroom	117
7. Problems and Possibilities	141
Notes	167
Selected Bibliography	171
Index	175

Preface

This is an exploratory study seeking to present complex arguments to a wider audience. Our understanding of speech, language, and consciousness is still evolving and needs further elaboration. Readers may find themselves dissatisfied with the linkage of the psychoanalytic concept of Otherness and Marxian class consciousness. They may wonder how the symbolic and imaginary functions of Lacanian psychoanalysis translate into the ideological thought and culture of capitalist systems. Some may insist that these are merely tangential elements of widely disparate systems. Nevertheless, such concepts as the voice of the Other and Otherness provide a link unifying the subjective theories of psychoanalysis with the objective ones of Marxism. By connecting thought, kinship structures, and ideological state apparatuses to speech and language, structural Marxists have bridged these discrete disciplines and given us new insight into ourselves and the intersubjective world we live in. Psychoanalysis, the talking cure, has become, first and foremost, a theory of communication and language. The concept of the Other has forced scholars to ponder more deeply the functions of speech and language in the development of human identity.

THE VOICE
OF THE OTHER

1

The Voice of the Other: An Introduction

Speech and language have become subjects of modern theoretical discourse. Once more the miracle of communication, performed without thought and with very little effort is seen as a key to understanding how the world of humans is possible. Even so, our grasp of these genetic and acquired characteristics presents us with seemingly insurmountable problems. Speech and language were pretty much neglected by the social sciences, with little attention being paid to them until the work of Ferdinand de Saussure, Roman Jakobson, and Jacques Lacan; but Sigmund Freud had mentioned verbal residues and word presentations as important areas of future research. No doubt some will say there is little reason to study something so diffuse and ambiguous, so closed to empirical investigation. But to concern ourselves with speech, and the ways people communicate, is not as inconsequential as it might at first appear. Communications must be studied through observations and descriptions, lending further support to the notion that scientific inquiries are really not possible. Imagine a scientist trying to describe a process that he cannot see, or sense in any way, a process that takes place without the subject's conscious awareness or effort! No, speech and language are too much a part of our genetic heritage to be subjects of serious inquiry and research.

And there are still other reasons why this may be so. In studying speech, we are not even sure of the object of our research or how it should be organized. A sentence, as an example, is spoken: "Teacher, may I leave the room?"

But what is there to study here, you may ask? As a rule, there is little to be gained by studying such mundane communications. If we query the student later, there is no way he can give an account of what he did prior to speaking the word "teacher." If he does give an account of his thoughts prior to speaking, do we have any assurance that he is correct, or that he may not have fabricated his account in order to provide a plausible explanation? Can we be sure his memory is good? And if so, do such memories include his unconsciousness and the unconscious of the other with whom he is speaking? Most talking is done without any conscious forethought: the individual hears and responds in a seemingly effortless manner.

These criticisms of the study of speech and language in human affairs are too strident. We know that on the surface the study of how we conduct such activities may seem unimportant. Yet it is often from such resistance-prone, commonplace behaviors that significant discoveries are made. As to the unconsciousness that attends the use of speech and language—that is one of the important characteristics of these behaviors and provides our first insight: speech and language are unconscious processes taking place without awareness. The subject matter seems too shapeless, too amorphous, for careful study. Yet if we return to the student who spoke the words, "Teacher, may I leave the room?," we can assume that a logical process of identification occurred before his words were uttered. This includes the construction of an Other who is separate and apart from the teacher who waits for the student to speak.[1] This Other is an imaginary construct that the student creates in order to think through what he wants to say and how he wants to say it to his listener. We can see that this concept also refers to the Otherness surrounding the student, providing him with understandings about his social situation and the possible responses to his spoken thoughts. We may, therefore, think this concept of the Other too inclusive and obscure for scientific discourse.

These negative responses to theoretical discourse seem to be a reaction to concepts that cannot be proved other than by observational and inferential methods. Any attempt to reconstruct a person's unconscious thought is a frustrating one at best, but we may assume that this Other of which we speak exists in every social situation wherein people interact. Interpreting such hidden processes means searching, in reverse, to see what suppositions and linguistic choices were probable in a given encounter.

The "Real" Other

We can best accomplish the above-stated goal by recalling how neonates first communicate their needs and desires. Ego psychologists have enumerated the ways infants interact with their attuned mothers prior to the acquisition of language. The Other in these early encounters signifies the parents of the newborn. Designated as the "real Other" is the mother, because of her exclusive relationship with the infant, while the father is the "symbolic Other" because he represents the social order and the world of language. Lacan believed there may have been times when these imaginary constructs were confused in the child's mind with the real world, but the Other was never to be understood as a person. It was always a means by which the infant attempted to orient himself to his new surroundings, developing suppositions about the Other and ways he could effectively communicate with his mother. When the Other was understood in this way, it almost always referred to the unconscious itself, the locus where speech and language reside. Both the mother and child need this third structure so they can test their suppositions and language before using them in actual sounds and speech. The value of this theoretical construct can be found in the ways it affects the communications of both the mother and child in their imaginary relationship. (The relationship is imaginary because it takes place in a world of linguistically labelled objects and persons who have been constructed in the image of the Other.) So the unconscious is conceived of as the Other, since it alone has the ability to allow human beings to gain access to language and to speak.

We must continue in the task of defining the Other, as this concept aids the individual, first and foremost, in finding his place in the imaginary world of the language and symbols that pervade human affairs.² The first thing common to all communications, as we have mentioned, is their unconsciousness. Speech is apparently a mental process that is carried on auto-pilot—something the individual has no idea he is doing until the words are heard. But the individual is always searching for an understanding of his social situation; he is always trying to understand others who are interacting with him. This, then, is an important function that the Other performs effortlessly for him. It may be that, as the child matures, his ego takes over the role of perceiving and understanding the object world and his relations to it. We have a great deal of research that points in this direction; we very often attribute to the ego and superego behaviors that were modified because an individual was able to weigh the consequences of other, more impulsive actions. But the Other is not a physical apparatus inside the mind; rather, it is the locus of the linguistic code individuals use to communicate thoughts, feelings, and moral understandings of the moment. Before the student in our example can speak the word "teacher," he must conjure up the image of the Other in the classroom setting; he must reorient himself to the status hierarchy and mores of classroom life; and he must choose words that will be received and understood by the teacher in accordance with his intentions. Can you imagine what it would be like if the student and his teacher spoke different languages? Communication would be very difficult indeed. For communication to work effectively, senders and receivers must decipher signification codes they hold in common. So the unconscious, in these instances, is nothing more or less than the discourse that individuals have with an imaginary Other before they speak to one another. Perhaps we have already said this, but it bears repeating. If a student wishes to be understood, he must be concerned with the linguistic and cultural background of his receiving person. Without the receiver's ability to receive and decode the sender's words, no meaningful communication is possible. Every schoolteacher in multicultural classroom settings has learned this important rule. So we can conclude by saying that the Other plays a powerful, controlling role in the thought and behavior of teachers and students, as one example. Their choice of words and messages is limited by these linguistic codes and imaginary constructs of the Other, and their sense of their receiver's abilities to decode them.

What, then, is the Other, we may ask again in growing frustration? It is an unconscious third entity in human communications that contains the language from which words are chosen for speech. It is also the way that the intersubjective world of families, classrooms, and social systems is made possible. But that is not all. We must understand that the unconscious and the Other are discourses that relay the cultural heritage and moral understandings of civilizations and classes through language. The Other is the third element in the duality existing between communicators. There are immense difficulties in grasping this clearly. The essential idea is that the unconscious of the individual student or teacher is never an intrapsychic feature of human thought. Rather, it is to be understood as a function of the social order that establishes and maintains it.

So we must repeat that the Other is the unconscious or thirdness in human communications that occurs between persons communicating with one another. The Other is the scene of the Word, because the Word is always in a third position between people who wish to speak to one another. The first thing common to all speech is that the speaker must locate himself in a particular situation. In our earlier example, this is the classroom where a student is seeking recognition. Speaking in such situations is a privilege and must be granted by the teacher. She alone has the right to decide who will be heard and who will listen in the classroom, and this right is steeped in tradition and in the organizational structures of schools. The student needs to take these things into account, even as he raises his hand and speaks the word "teacher." He must construct an imaginary Other of the teacher, one that will permit him to select words and sentences that convey his message effectively. This unconscious selection of words gives intentionality to his message; by selecting some words and not others, his speech takes on a special significance and meaning. Thus, the thoughts and actions of teachers and students are influenced by the imaginary, symbolic world of the school. Even if the student thinks and speaks to himself, the Other exists, choosing the words in language that can best be understood by him. But the symbolic encompasses more than this: it is also the "world of rules" and "symbolic relationships" into which individuals are born and learn to adapt in spite of their innermost drives and impulses.

This, then, is the concept Lacan used to explain how the world of intersubjectivity is possible. The Other is related to discourses that relay cultural norms, heritages, and moral understandings from one generation to the next.[3] On this we can agree readily enough, but we ought to describe further the ways in which this concept maintains and reproduces the social order. The Other is an imaginary construct that the individual knows nothing about; he cannot bring it to consciousness even when he tries, even when it is orienting him to his situation and the people in it. We activate the Other by perceiving another and speaking to him. We also activate it when we think quietly about another. So when we speak, we say, "Who is this Other? What does he want from me?" The psychological purpose of the Other seems to be that of a sounding board in these circumstances, and its primary characteristic is the use of language to understand others and the object world. Our relation to others seems to involve a need to construct and define verbally an unconscious Other before we choose the words we speak. Thus, we speak the words that have been chosen from the Other without being conscious of how we accomplished this feat. In any case, we turn to the Other to find the words, because the Word is always the defining element in the symbolic world of humans. The world of our thoughts, it seems, is expressed primarily in words and spoken sentences with the Other prior to actual speech. Indeed, in thinking about our conversations after they have occurred, we often say that we used the right or wrong word to express a certain thought. (In saying this, we acknowledge the powerful role words play in constructing the social reality within which we live.) We speak, also, of "reading" another so that we know precisely what he is thinking or feeling at a given moment.

The First Human Order

If this is what communication is, the Other must be in evidence in the beginning when babies and parents first try to make themselves understood. The family is the first human order, unconsciously relaying cultural and moral understandings to the child. There ought to be intelligible sounds voiced by the participants; if a child stirs or cries, we can expect the attuned mother to come to his side; although she may not be able to interpret everything the infant is communicating since his cries may signify many needs or anxieties. But there is a parental need to make sense of a baby's vocalizations. It is assumed that the neonate has needs and concerns; he is, after all, a human being with the genetic abilities to communicate with others of his species. Already, the parent has constructed an Other that defines the child in language. But if the child has no language, how can he speak and how can he understand? He cannot make his innermost thoughts and impulses clear, but he can communicate a great deal to the attuned mother. So it really is no surprise that these two initially establish a private language. Later, the child becomes more aware of the words signifying objects and desires; as his ego matures, he also becomes more aware of his environment and the words and language his parents use to communicate with him.

Even before the infant was born, however, he was predefined by an intersubjective, symbolic network that predetermined much of his social identity and destiny. Why does this symbolic order have such power over the lives of individuals? Probably because the idea of an individual psychology is untenable. Social stimuli act upon the infant from birth, and, more and more, he is forced to attend to them. An individual's psychological orientations are formed in these first social structures that are constructed in language and constitute the symbolic order. And here we see how the primacy of the social over the psychological is crystallized in the psychoanalytical concept of the Other. It is through the Other that parents initially speak of the infant rather than to him. It is through this Other that parents relay the culture and language of their family and class position to their child.

Is this, then, the beginning of the infant's intersubjective world? Yes, but it begins in this natural mode and develops, over time, into the more complicated, human symbolic order. The newborn hears the voice of the Other and comes to know it as the attuned mother who responds to his needs. He experiences her primarily through images, touches, and sounds; emotions are present also, and desires may take form, yet the first relations between these two are focused around their desire to communicate. The difficulty is that the unconsciousness of both is in the process of creating a common, primitive signification code. "I can understand everything he is saying," a mother often says, "but now and then he seems to cry for no reason." This is a period during which Otherness is bound up with the identity that the infant and mother possess in their imaginary relationship: it is imaginary, though both of the participants perceive it as taking place in the real world. Although they do not understand this world of symbols they quickly create, they do become aware of the ground rules it sets for their thoughts and actions. One outgrowth of this process is the initial maturing unconscious of the infant as his psychic and perceptual abilities improve, as he begins his journey from the natural order to the symbolic one. Much occurs that cannot be properly vocalized, however, as the infant suffers discomfort, frustration, and rage. His unconscious learns to deal with feelings of ambivalence and worse, and the first evidences of an ego emanating from the id appear. The words that act as signifiers appear as well, as do signified features of the world around him. But as he interacts with his mother, language is mastered or, as Lacan says, language masters the child. It is through the Other that the first human communications are made; it is through the Other, too, that more sophisticated messages are sent once the child becomes proficient in his use of language. The child will respond to more and more stimuli in his environment, though it will take some time before he reacts to social and cultural pressures.

Are there other events that happen in these early years? We can see that the Other becomes a central concern from the first. It controls the infant's first associations with his parents and forces him to attend to the world, teaching him to see it in terms of logic, rules, and orderliness. Yet even language acquisition is slowed by the biological needs of the infant to sleep.[4] As the infant's sleeping and waking patterns evolve, he begins to perceive and acquire, to touch and see, to smell, and so on. The measure of his comfort still depends upon the feeding experience, during which time he and his mother seem merged, and he finds it difficult to distinguish between himself and the Other who takes care of him. Language becomes more important, determining to a large extent whether the relationship is predominantly positive and cooperative or not. But the absence of verbal ability limits the discourse, as we indicated earlier, and the baby's cries are sometimes open to misunderstandings. "I think he's hungry," a mother is often heard to say, trying to anticipate or understand the sounds her baby makes. There are sounds that come to be recognizable, so clear to the attuned mother that she answers the baby's needs without thinking about them. Indeed the limited choice of messages becomes ever wider as the two struggle to make themselves understood. Communications may be entirely sensible at first; at other times, they may be confused and unintelligible. There are sounds that leave the mother baffled and others she thinks she understands, vocalizations that are received in confusion and panic and others that make it clear that both mother and child have little control over how their messages are being received. Thoughts may appear in the infant, but they are relayed to the mother in a language that has not yet mastered pronunciation and syntax.[5]

Toward the end of the first year of life, the infant's ability to send intentional messages improves. Since crying was one of the first and easiest vocalizations, it becomes a part of the expressive language the infant uses to gain the attention of the Other. But the child still does not possess a distinct sense of himself and others; his acceptance of the reality principle is at best fragmentary. Slowly the ego functions needed for complex verbalizations develop, and he becomes better able to express his intentions. His relationships with others become more symbolic, and he becomes more conscious of the familial relations of people living in his house. His speech patterns improve. Yet his first vocalizations often fail to express his thoughts and feelings adequately. The word "moma" is formed by movements of the jaw that are close to those of instinctual sucking. But the meaning behind this word may include declarations of discomfort, hunger, fear, or anxiety. At times, the infant may simply connect these vocalizations with certain mental images he is experiencing at the moment. As the child matures, his mastery of language shows itself in the pronouncement of grammatically correct sentences, but his ability to convey emotions is still absent. He begins to discover the power of negative statements and uses them to assert his individuality and newly acquired power to upset the Other. At this stage, the most important feature of discourses is their transsubjectivity. They provide the infant with a tie to the social world, relaying the cultural consciousness of the family and society to the new generation. In this, Lacan agrees with Levi-Strauss that the unconscious is not an individual, intrapsychic phenomena but rather an outgrowth of the collectivity that creates and sustains it through language.[6]

The unconscious, then, is a communication system structured like a language but quite separate and apart from conscious speech. Yet the two are connected by their common attention to signifiers and the signified of the real world. There are words that are repressed during these early years and locate themselves in the unconscious because of the anxiety, fear, guilt, or shame they create in the maturing child. Indeed, the act of feeding, which arouses feelings of love, may also trigger feelings of dependency and hatred. The attuned mother may be late at times in responding to the infant's cries or inadvertently frustrate him in other ways; at other times, she may be distracted or worse. These are the experiences that create the first evidences of ambivalence in the child's mind, causing him to repress certain feelings that conflict with his love for the mothering person. Events and relationships are transcribed into language once the unconscious is able to do so. The unconscious may coexist with the speech of the child, with signifiers passing freely between them. In short, this second structure situates itself between the images and actions a child experiences and transposes them into intelligibility. Through language, the unconscious assures that events are inscribed in the mind and available for recall. It strengthens the symbolic perceptions of the infant even as many of these perceptions are repressed and so out of conscious reach and disposal.

We might try to account for these processes by recalling the impact language has on the prenatal and early moments of an infant's life. It is in language's mastery of the child that the Other becomes transformed into the collective unconsciousness that encodes the family's universalistic conception of itself and its class position in society. Interhuman communications through language teach the child who he is and where he fits in the social order. The code of language, through the unconscious, acts as a repository for the personal, tribal, and social myths of his world. Through this code, he learns who to like and dislike, what illusions and identifications to cherish, and what verbal constructions of reality to accept as real and true.

The symbolic and imaginary worlds of the child coexist during this period. Intersubjectivity, which is crucial to his survival and growth, is primarily a symbolic phenomena with the imaginary playing an important but undefined role. It is difficult to say what the ability to use language means to the young child except that it provides him with the power to speak in the first person and to make his needs known more clearly. The child is born outside of the symbolic order of his parents, but he is immediately confronted by its effects. The important question, as he matures, becomes one of self-identity: "Who (or what) am I?" Language gives him access to the highly complex symbolic structures of the social order. But the child cannot pose these questions without becoming aware of his relationships with significant others. He is the son of this person, the brother of that one, and so on.

The Other, then, can be understood in many ways but it always implies a thirdness or Otherness to which the discourse of the infant is initially directed. It is essentially found in the Word, because the Word is always between communicators. It can be the mother or, symbolically, the father. And it is from this Other that the child learns what verbal descriptions and characterizations are applied to himself. It is through the words that others use that the child learns to see himself, thus committing the first and most important act of misrecognition. He comes to see the words of others as his inner self, mistaking them for his central core or being.

Speech and Language

What is the relationship between speech and language? How are they different? We inferred earlier that both are unconscious processes. We also know that speech is an act of signification and that words are signifiers requiring decoding if communication is to occur. Many investigators of these phenomena have deduced that language is the symbolic reality that binds humanity together in an intersubjective world. The infant in our earlier example can serve us again: he was given a name, a race, and a class position before he was born. He learned to interact with others and mastered the words and syntax needed for complex communications. He was forced to being a journey from the natural order of his birth to a symbolic one; he understood, at last, the words that were applied to him and his behavior. After a number of years, his self-identity was clearly set; he was an American boy, of Jewish parents, living in a large city in the Northeast.

The striking thing about language is its universality. It exists and is the same no matter who uses it. It is a universe unto itself, pretending to encompass and explain everything that exists in the world. These descriptions are sensible enough and have the concreteness and coherence of linguistic constructions. What needs to be added is the component of speech, which is intensely personal and ego-centered. Only the spoken (or written) word can signify, and it can do this only in the context of a commonly held language and culture. It is through the spoken word that the attuned mother transmits the social identity of the family to her child, but this already exists in the language they share. Of course, signifiers can have many meanings, but the sentences the mother speaks fix her meanings within the framework of their relationship. Ambiguities are further resolved by the continual use of words or utterances.

And now consider this mother-infant relationship more closely. In most cases, both seek to transmit messages to one another, indicating their intentions. At times, they may become confused, especially when the child begins to send more complicated messages. Yet the attuned mother usually persists and is able to understand her infant. "Angie baba!" a child says, confidently. His mother hears and understands: "Empty bottle!" The infant has learned the language in which these words make sense, though he has not yet learned to pronounce them clearly. He has been able to construct an Other and to choose words his mother will hear and understand. He is alive in a world of symbols that appear to accurately reflect and apprehend his surroundings.

The child slowly learns the universal discourse of his people, traveling from his natural state at birth to a more complex, cultural one. He locates himself in his family, neighborhood, and so on, and finds that he has a predetermined social identity. These insights lead to others: he learns to present himself as he has been recorded in language. These linguistic definitions of his self determine how others will see and respond to him even before they meet and know him. To repeat, the infant was located in the symbolic world before he was born. His mother and father spoke of him and named him; his birth was a message to the world; his possibilities in life were limited by his proclaimed social identity. In other words, the infant enters a world of signs and symbols that are entirely apart from himself. Yet this world contains undifferentiated words whose meanings are ambiguous until they are used in actual speech. It is only then that the race or sex of the child becomes an advantage or an impediment, depending on the social situation of the family. Words may have several meanings, but these are clarified in the speech of the sender and receiver of messages. Still, language must be mastered, since it is the enabler that allows speech to occur. It presents us with the possibility of temporal reality and allows us to think of ourselves as part of a concrete, orderly universe. The linguist Saussure must be given the credit for this separation of speech from language.[7] He was one of the first to differentiate between the sign, the signifier, and the signified. For him, language was a universal system of signs containing the social and collective values and folklore of society. These were outside the control or consciousness of the individual and opposed to the act of speech. Speech was a conscious use of linguistic structures, which were unconsciously determined by still other structures and determinations, or what we have termed the Other, in the Lacanian sense. Saussure understood that speech and language were inseparably bound to one another and in constant interaction. Indeed, languages have grown and evolved through speech, which has constantly shaped them according to the new needs and concerns of speakers. The value of the Other, then, was that it clarified how intersubjective communication was possible and how it functioned from one person to another, from one generation to another. The social code of a system was transmitted through language, providing infants with the moral and social understandings of their families. Individual messages were forced to conform to the assumptions of a language speakers used without conscious effort, thus placing a third entity between themselves and those to whom they spoke.

Saussure, who developed new ways of thinking about languages, argued that they should be studied with an awareness of their historical development. For instance, in studying the language of a primitive tribe in New Zealand, it was important to remember that this language was probably in a late stage of development. His interpretation was based on the historical period in which the study was taking place, a period far removed from primitive languages spoken by prehistoric people. Similarly, the words used by speakers needed to be understood in their evolution, as they were used by people in their daily lives.

Structural anthropologists[8] co-opted these ideas, using them to study societies in different stages of social and historical development. Primitive societies were thought to be synchronic in their essence, with little awareness of history other than the oral stories, folklore, and great events that were passed on by elders. These societies also relied on a few learned men who were able to transmit the myths and sacred beliefs of the tribe. The speaker spoke the words of others from the past, adding as little as possible to the story itself. More advanced social systems were seen as players in the saga of human history, even though they were often mired in traditional myths and cultures. In the advanced societies, writing provided an objective memory that could be passed on more easily.

Levi-Strauss was concerned with uncovering and comparing cultures and languages and showed little interest in how these were changed by speech. Rather, he concentrated on the ways that social systems were structured by language and how they acted and reacted on new generations, holding society together. While they paralleled those of others, Levi-Strauss was careful to indicate how his usages of these terms differed from those of structural linguists.[9] For the anthropologist, two sets of linguistic categories were in opposition: those that dealt with grammar, the synchronic, the conscious; and those of phonetics, the diachronic, and the unconscious. Following Freud, Levi-Strauss indicated that only the conscious system was rational or "coherent"; the unconscious was dynamic and psychological, carrying within it the past legacies and future possibilities of the culture. Saussure seemed unaware of the hidden realities of these unconscious structures and believed they could be studied through observation. Levi-Strauss began to see these opposing categories as elements of an inseparable entity, with both a conscious and unconscious apparatus. He saw, along with Marx, that speech's evolution contained within it a social language of culture and class; and he agreed with Freud that the syntax of speech could flower in the heart of what is personal.

Every group has symbolic functions that are internalized by its members who accept them at birth. For Lacan, familial communications are primary and unconscious discourses. The unconscious is, as Lacan discovered, "structured as a language," because it is the locus of the Word, and in the Word, speech and communication are made possible. The idea includes the notion of language as an enabler of the Word, which is sometimes in the preconscious or unconscious structures of the mind. The unconscious interferes with the discourse of the individual, accounting for the distortions and discontinuities in his communications. We can think of the person as an unconscious subject who is unaware of these barred remembrances. Nevertheless, this unconscious part of the subject seeks to communicate itself to the unconsciousness of the Other. Lacan is unclear about whether the unconscious is a discourse between persons or simply structured like a language, allowing for both interpretations according to the depth of the unconscious being explored. But the distorted signifiers and signs of the dream imply a censor that stands between the conscious and unconscious, deciding which ideas and impulses will be admitted to consciousness and which will not. The dream allows the thoughts and emotions of the subject's earliest years to reach the surface during sleep, but in distorted and condensed forms and perceptions. When the dreamer tries to understand the images in his dream, he is forced to remember and to interpret them in words. Thus, what he actually interprets is the verbal remembrance of the dream and not the dream itself. His discourse is with the Other within himself, structuring his thought and expression according to the rules and syntaxes of language. The interpretations are valid because the spoken words reflect the same distortions and defensive responses that occurred in the dream itself. Interpretation of these censored reveries leads to an understanding of those that were in the dream. The dreamer, or the person to whom he is addressing his remarks, now becomes a substitute for the significant other who germinated the dream in the first instance.

Psychological Dimensions

The effects of an infant's first identifications (or cathexes) are generic and long lasting. They lead us back to Freud's notion that the Oedipal period in a child's development is crucial; for behind it there exists the individual's first journey from the natural to the Symbolic order, his first identification with the symbolic father and his own history and culture. This is a consequence of his mastery of language; it is a direct and immediate result of the infant's earlier identification with his mother, and especially his mother's breast.[10] But this object-choice seems harmless enough in the earliest days of the child's life, and the father is seen as an imaginary and symbolic Other who is not to be feared or envied. The relationships between these three are relatively benign at first. Then, at an early age, the little boy, as one example, comes to identify more intensely with his mother; his sexual urges become more apparent, and he comes to see his father as a rival and obstacle. Until this moment, the boy tended to identify himself with his father. But with the advent of the Oedipus complex, his attitudes toward his father become more hostile, and he wishes to be rid of this parent so that he can "take his place with his mother." This results in a sometimes confrontational relationship with his father, and it seems that the little boy enters into an imaginary rivalry, one in which this parent holds all the advantages. Only now does the child begin to perceive the external dangers that threaten him; only now does he develop a realistic sense of anxiety in the face of his demanding impulsiveness. It is true that the symbolic father can be an object of his son's aggressiveness for a time. To the boy, the father is a real danger because of his love for his mother and the possibility of punishment if his true feelings were to become known. The danger, as Freud discovered in his clinical work, is the fear of castration, or losing the genital organ.[11]

Over time, the boy's relationship to his father begins to change, and it seems as if he slowly realizes that he must give up his sexual wishes toward his mother. Henceforth his relationship to his father becomes one of intensified identification or ambivalence; this outcome, and a feeling of a more affectionate kind toward his mother, is considered a positive resolution of the Oedipus complex.

Returning to the anxiety created by the boy's sexual feelings toward his mother, we can wonder if such fears are valid, since castration is not a common practice or occurrence in contemporary society. Of course this is true. But Freud also introduced a third element into these relationships, that of the phallus—an imaginary symbol of considerable significance. Since the phallus exists only in the imaginary world, it is linked to unconscious fantasies and demands. In ancient Greece, it was seen as an insignia or the most important of all significations. In mythology and in psychoanalysis, it represents the penetration or vital force that cannot enter the mind of the signifier without being repressed by it, without conjuring up fears of castration. At this level, the symbolic father is the Other, an Other who is capable of wreaking a terrible vengeance on his sinful son.

In its most essential form, the phallus is a feature of the symbolic social order into which the infant is born. At a very early age, the little boy meets it in the object world; he does not imagine this "object." For a time he becomes identified with it because of the attuned mother who forces him to accept the identity and behavioral patterns of this important Other. His fear of castration at the hands of his father, who represents the law and the rule of the stronger, also affects his identity formation during the resolution of the Oedipal complex. The curbing of incestuous urges is paramount if the child is to make the choices that secure his relationships with both parents and the social order in which he lives. His mastery of language permits him to enter the symbolic order; through his displacement and identification with the rival parent of his sex, he emerges as a social person. Henceforth his relation to language is determinate, as it helps him to differentiate between his needs and impulses, between his erotic desires and the strictures of social life. The Word, as a part of language, becomes an overpowering force in his life, interpreting his relationships with others and with the object world. It becomes, in many instances, a way of remembering, a way of making sense of past events.

You will not be surprised if we end this section with a further discussion of the unconscious. The unconscious, as Freud discovered, is the inaccessible part of our consciousness; what we know of it is that it is transindividual and does not relate to the individual's sense of reality alone. We approach the unconscious by seeking past evidences of its existence: we call it a history of the individual's forgotten past, a dark space that has been censored by a stern and invisible hand. We seek its truth, not alone in remembrances at first, but in monuments or behavioral relics that have survived and that include the structure of language and modes of deciphering our past and present. The unconscious is our forgotten childhood memories, the source of which is unknown to us. Its characteristics are to be sought in the semantic development of the subject, and this includes the way he uses words to shape his life and self-identity. Further evidences can be discovered in the traditions of families and peoples as well, and in the stories of family heroes relayed from the past. At the most, they converge to form a linguistic tradition that shapes the subject's history. There is, finally, the preserved traces of the unconscious—the distortions that have developed as a consequence of childhood traumas whose meanings are now beyond the subject's grasp. There is in the unconscious the laws of history and nations and the ideas of civilization. Past events are crystallized in language and transmitted orally before they are finally written down. For the individual, the unconscious is his personal history, containing every shame and scar. These forgotten spaces are recalled in the actions and behaviors of the subject now; after the passage of many years they still have their psychic power and energy.

The unconscious knows and organizes the instinctual stages

through which an individual lives. No happening is forgotten or ignored. The developmental accomplishments of the infant are duly chronicled and include the training of his bowel movements and the imaginary sexual experiences he associates with his orifices. These stages are purely historical phenomena when they are reconstituted in analysis or in sudden instances of remembrance. It seems that again and again the unconscious is the discourse of the Other. The world is interpreted for the individual in words that provide him with a universe of understanding, and these derive their meanings from language and its usage in transsubjective communications.

In the unconscious, we find the Other and Otherness existing as a third party in interhuman communications. This third party is imaginary and symbolic in the same moment, but without the recognition and desire of this Other, meaningful messages would be impossible. Words introduce the symbolic system into the process of communication, allowing both speaker and listener to see and know one another and the social situation within which they meet. The system of exchanges are found here, as are the social structures that were formed in the past and now shape present-day encounters. Teachers and students, as one example, know how to act and react to one another, not because of their knowledge of the classroom situation but because of their recognition of it.

The ego and alter ego structure such encounters, using symbolic and imaginary functions to construct the pedagogic moment. Ambiguity and ambivalence suffuse these coercive engagements, as teachers and students find themselves confused and deeply troubled by the conflicts and contradictions of classroom life.

From the moment that they enter into discourse, teachers and students see themselves as subjects, as doers, as the "I" that experiences and interprets the real world. They do not see themselves as one of many participating in the pedagogic work of state schools. Rather, they experience classroom routines on an intensely personal level. They cannot do otherwise, since their self-consciousness sees the world as revolving around them, as having no reality until it is discovered and recognized by them. They cannot visualize themselves as part of the unity of the pedagogic situation. For them, each moment is happening "out there" where they can see and hear it.

Sociocultural Perspectives

We must now make a sudden turn and attempt to answer a question that seems unavoidable: is the social supreme over the psychological in the formation of the self?

Cultural and linguistic heritages are core concepts in the social sciences and raise difficult problems. If we try to define these terms, we are forced to make many exceptions. Nevertheless, it is our conviction that these concepts are the symbolic constructions that relay the past of the family and society to future generations. It can be easily understood that the language of parents fixes the child to his social and cultural place in the symbolic order from birth. Accepting these ideas, the infant can feel secure in his immediate surroundings and relationships; he can know what to value and what to turn away from, and how to deal with his own emotions and those of others around him.

This ascendancy of the social over the psychological was first expressed in the work of Marcel Mauss. It was his belief that the genesis of the self evolved from the symbolic relationships that developed between the newborn and his parents.[12] Cultural and symbolic expressions had a special place in the transmission of the customs, mores, and moral understandings of a society. Their contributions to the self systems of youth lay precisely in the symbolic system and collectivity that the newborn faced at birth. And, as was mentioned earlier, these symbolic expressions existed before the infant was conceived; his later, autonomous actions were structured and defined by the language he and his parents had inherited.

Of the writers who supported and widened the scope of these ideas, Levi-Strauss was the most important. He set forth the precise structure and nature of these cultural, symbolic kinship systems. Language is almost always to be understood as decisive; it alone establishes the marriage rules, economic relationships, art, science, and religion of a people. Cultural systems, which are created by human beings, are accomplished and enclosed in a world of symbols; these are always established within the rules of language, constituting, in the final analysis, the ways in which the universe can be grasped by individuals. The rules of marriage contain preferences and prohibitions that have changed considerably in modern times. Yet they continue to be formed in a symbolic order, presenting themselves as representations in a formal, complete universalistic system. And these symbolic orders are found in all societies, relaying themselves through language from one generation to the next. They envelop the infant from the beginning in a web of social, economic, and political hierarchies.

If we are to understand the importance of language, we must bear in mind what it undertakes to do for the human order; we must see it as the transmitter of a person's class position in capitalist society. It alone gives the newborn knowledge of his family culture and estate, and it also assures him of its support during his most dependent period. Thus, it establishes the infant as an object in the symbolic system long before he can reasonably take his place as a subject or "I"; it does this before he can acquire the linguistic skills he will need to become a functioning individual. It is in its formalization of marriage rules that language makes its unique contribution to the state power in modern capitalist states, providing a powerful ideological apparatus that transmits to the new generation information about the child's social and economic relationships. Economic relations determine the class position of the newborn's family and their attitudes toward art, science, religion, diet, and even toward strangers. It is true that later learnings can alter some of these earliest teachings, but it seems foolish to ignore the power of such transmissions and their instinctive conservatism.

The relationships between parents and children are governed by transmissions that depend entirely upon symbolic functions. What has this to do with their day-to-day relationships? The need to make their intentions known to one another is constant, assuring society that they will seek rational forms of communication based on the language of their ancestors. They have no other way of sending and receiving messages. Only those who learn the language of the culture will benefit from their development; punishment and disgrace await those unfortunates who, for one reason or another, are unable to make the transition from the natural to the cultural order. Of course, the infant is trying to identify with others who are outside his mind and body. How can he unite his thoughts and feelings with those of his parents? How can he communicate the uncommunicable, uniting the subjective in some external objectivity?

Again, the remarkable work of Marcel Mauss can help us answer these vexing questions. They may be approached from the most original of his thoughts—his view of the unconscious mind as an extradimensional category that contained the collective thought of a people. The unconscious transmitted through the mediation of parents allowed the two subjectivities to become as one. It mediated between their selves and one another, finding its highest development once a common language was established between them. It is an interesting fact that mothers often communicate with their infants before the infant learns to use language; their common activities make their actions and needs more comprehensible than they might otherwise be. It is also true that the infant's emotional states are usually misrecognized by the attuned mother, since these cannot be accurately transmitted. For Levi-Strauss, the knowledge that was gained in these communications was always objective even as they sometimes transcended language and led to subjective interpretations. The problem of the infant identifying with the Other was solved at the unconscious level of human interaction, with language acting as the mediator of last resort. As the child learned language, he became a subjective "me" and also an object of a significant other; he developed an understanding of the differences between "me" and the individual who was the other in his first relationships.

A number of questions about these encounters are bothersome. It seems as though we are witnessing a psychological fusion, a genetic coming together of two individuals. The child appears to be able to take over the role of the Other for a moment, enabling him to presuppose what the attuned other will do in response to his cries. The dimension of intersubjectivity is an unstated presumption and is confirmed by the child's awareness that he is engaged with an Other. The variations in his comfort and safety depend upon his ability to make himself known to this indispensable other.

This being so, it is all the more important for the newborn to overcome his difficulty in differentiating himself from the Other. There seems little doubt that the infant assumes that the Other is thinking what he thinks during their communications with one another. This is because he supposed that the nurturing Other will not fail to feed him once the message of hunger is conveyed successfully. There will come a moment when this Other is late in responding to his cries, creating the first signs of ambivalence in his emotional life, but seldom will she fail to respond at all. At a later stage in his development, the child will be able to take the place of the Other, to think like her; he will learn to imagine this thirdness as a separate entity that exists between himself and his mother.

That the infant should think the Other similar, that he should assume a commonality in their thinking, tells us little enough about their first psychological experiences together since much of it occurs in the realm of the imaginary. Only by examining the language that comes into use can we begin to understand the reflexive positions of these first encounters. Only then can we comprehend the child's first recognition of the Other's existence and his understanding that he, too, is an Other for her.

2
Language and Thought

We cannot consider the newborn's emerging self-consciousness without attending to his speech and language. Two stages seem important to us: the origins of self-consciousness when the infant learns to communicate his need for recognition, and the words he learns to associate with the Other and with Otherness. We have to consider these in their turn, for they have been widely reported elsewhere.[1] If we examine these studies closely, we find that they agree that speech and language develop in an intensely personal way. Before the infant learns to speak the language of his family, he communicates in a personalized idiom; as parents provide a safe haven and interact with him, he learns the concepts of the Other and of Otherness. Primal needs of recognition and communication exist from the first moments of consciousness, leading to eventual separation and self-awareness. These will be affected, in time, by the acquisition of language and the discovery of self-identity in the discourse of others. The self now becomes a product of thought and language, autonomous and a part of the abstractions comprising the symbolic world of humans.

Three psychogenetic processes help the child organize his sensory perceptions during these early experiences: the mirror or reflective, the imaginary, and the symbolic. We already know that the reflective refers to the images streaming into the child's consciousness. This leads to the imaginary function, which explains these worldly images and the child's relationships with others. Finally, the symbolic mediates these cognitive apperceptions, signifying and ordering them through word presentations.

It seems important to say another word or two about these organizing processes. They all respond to sensory perceptions of the mind, providing egotistical and self-centered perceptions for individuals. But what are the reasons for these egocentric, organizing processes? Simply put, they fulfill a primal need for recognition and protection against an alien and hostile world. The difference between the real object and its mental image consists of this: the former is materially there, whereas the latter exists only in the specular, imaginary, and symbolic world of the mind.

Let us consider further the child's emerging sense of himself and his task of acquiring speech and language in the first years of his life. Initially, he is consumed by the mother-child relationship; later he learns to associate with siblings and others in his immediate vicinity. Relations with these others are influenced by his dependent physical, social, and psychological condition. Instances of hostility between infants and mothers (and siblings) are something everyone has experienced in their personal lives. But it is also true that a great many of the child's earliest feelings of anger and frustration are internalized and repressed, disappearing into an unremembered unconsciousness.

This Otherness with which the infant seeks to deal is often the world in a philosophical sense, developing in complexity at different stages in his life. The older child becomes aware of a wider universe as his body matures, while the younger is consumed with confusion, rage, and moments of psychic and physical satisfaction derived primarily from the ministering parent. His internalizations of the emerging universe provide the infant with a sense of the rules and regulations, allowing him to enter into an increasingly wider social circle.

In these earliest moments, as we have already mentioned, children are completely self-centered; they feel a compulsion to be recognized and try desperately to satisfy this need—especially since their lives depend upon an ability to galvanize the nurturing Other into action when they are hungry or soiled. It is in these first associations that the child comes to exert his own personality and separation from the significant other who cares for him. And it is then that G.W.F. Hegel's idea of the role of alienation in the development of self-consciousness emerges.[2]

All human beings are a part of nature, as they have been born with genetic drives, capabilities, and tendencies that structure much of their emerging self-consciousness. Nevertheless, these natural creatures suffer, as do all living things, because of the limitations of sensory and intellectual organs. The objects humans see and desire live outside themselves in a real and independent world they can only know as images and symbols. Yet these objects are often required if they are to survive and confirm themselves. The fact that human beings are animals living and working in a natural world tests their genetic capabilities and forces them to express themselves in terms of an Otherness that exists outside themselves. They learn to satisfy hunger and other desires—natural needs that they cannot easily deny. This forces them to seek and acquire objects outside themselves and to learn that, for other species and individuals, they can become an object, too.

At this point, we must ask ourselves some Hegelian questions: How does the neonate and infant "know" the world around him? How does he develop self-consciousness? We can explain these phenomena by focusing upon the images that enter into the consciousness of the child in a diverse and uncensored stream—that is, the natural world as it appears to the infant.

Initially, the material world can be known by individuals only through their self-consciousness. We know from Hegel's experiments that sensory perceptions can be further differentiated into natural revelations at the moment when objects become a focus of attention, entering a person's stream of consciousness and reappearing as a focused image in the mind. In the act of cognition, individuals know the image of the object. The real is perceived only through this medium of imagery and later in the symbolic world in which humans live. The object appears to move toward the knowing person and into consciousness, seeming to take the place of the observed object and rendering the image real for him.

The fact that human beings are essentially egocentric, natural animals concerned primarily with their own needs and desires, is a conclusion so unremarkable that we will mention it only in passing. Hegel tells us further that the perceptions of objects in the real world appear to return to the self when they enter a person's self-consciousness. The individual knows nothing about the real object, not even that it has become an image in his mind. What is more, to conjure up this mental image, to think about it or to speak about it, as we shall see later in this chapter, is impossible without invoking the imaginary and symbolic functions of the mind. The imaginary promotes the perceptions and understandings of the unauthenticated and unknowable parts of the world and universe. It operates as an illogical mechanism of the mind, producing order and sense out of a generally disorderly and senseless world. This is distinguished from, but intimately tied to, the symbolic order, which is constructed of the linguistic and discursive actions of individuals. It is in language that the infant learns to identify his self, imagining the words for his own inner core; it is in language that he learns to "understand" his world and the world of others. The Real, in this instance, is merely what is real for him.

Thus, individuals consist of themselves and their consciousness. They cannot know themselves except through understandings that come to them through their stream of consciousness; they cannot know what is real in any direct way other than by transforming objects into images. Following Hegel, then, we can say that the newborn's life begins when he perceives himself as a separate entity from the Otherness about him. At first, this is primarily a sensual and tactile process. The breast, or feeding object, is seen or felt and enters into consciousness as though it were a part of him; later, as vision improves, it will seem to travel inward toward his innermost self. In time, the child will learn to focus his eyes on particular objects that will then pass from their natural state into his stream of consciousness. At this point, the object will have both a positive and a negative significance for him and his consciousness; it will exist in its natural state and in his emerging consciousness as an image or reflection. (Again, that which is real for him is not what is actually real but merely what he comes to believe is real.) It is the appearance of the object that he comes to know, not the object itself. Its essence is hidden and distorted by the limitations of the person's consciousness and his symbolic understandings of the world.

It is in the writings of Hegel that the idea of the individual's alienation from himself and others first appeared, planting the seed from which the ideas of Martin Heidegger, Edmund Husserl, and Jacques Lacan flowered. They purported a phenomenological basis for understanding how the world was perceived by humans, while providing insight into the individual's shift from a natural stage at birth to a civilized one capable of speech and language at about age three. If this process fails to develop, we cannot talk of the formation of the self, and serious mental illness seems sure to follow. After the separation and self-consciousness of the child have begun, the experiences are neither natural nor harmonious, as Freud's discoveries of the familial complexes have shown us. There is need for the infant to become opposed to himself, rediscovering his self through a separation that permits him to make himself an object of reflection in the symbolic world.[3]

Hegel's dialectic in the *Phenomenology of Mind*[4] asserts that the infant recognizes, misrecognizes, and becomes aware of objects in the surrounding world. His consciousness of these others permits him to attain a sense of himself, especially when he recognizes and is recognized by significant others. He learns that his self is an other for others, developing an intersubjective communication and cognition and reconciling his dual roles of self and other in order to take his place in the social and symbolic world of his family. He learns to identify himself first as the self that demands recognition and sustenance and then as the other in a dialectical relationship.

This discourse between the child and his parent sets the boundaries for his emerging self-consciousness. Through experiences of gratification, denial, and repression, the child moves toward individuality and the absolute subjectivity that accompanies his entrance into the world of words and symbols. Thus, the moment in which desire or need compels the emerging self-consciousness of the infant to cry out begins the journey from nature to civilized being. When the child cries out in the night, he does not do so merely to overcome his discomfort or to satisfy a desire. His actions cause the attuned mother to recognize him and to appear as if by magic. And this process of primitive communication leads inevitably to membership in the child's familial and cultural group. He listens to the ongoing discourses of family members, involving himself by the assertive behavior he has learned from them.

If a child's wish for recognition propels him forward into family and social life, how can we explain the two persons he now becomes? A solution is provided by the observations that the natural self and alter ego both have a common need: both need to be recognized, using innate abilities of speech and language to develop social relations with others. In Hegel's *Phenomenology of Mind*, the object of the individual's wishes or desires is what dominates any relationship he has with others; desired objects and actions are understood only in relation to the shared symbolic understandings of those objects. Hence, the desired object of action is desired because of its usefulness and because it is something he has been taught to believe is desirable in itself. But the child's identification with Otherness around him, or with parts of objects, is the primitive stage of this process; his desire to become a part of this object (the mother's breast, as one instance) is evidence of his early inability to separate himself from the world of his birth.

Commenting on Hegel's *Phenomenology of Mind*, Alexandre Kojeve notes that the dialectic at the base of this philosophy does not exist in nature, which knows only positive principles.[5] Negativity is what human consciousness brings to the knowing equation through its desires, discourses, and speech, transposing the natural world into a symbolic one. Discourse provides the individual with a rational totality and explanation of the object world, but humans and nature do not operate on the same "ontological" principle. Nature knows nothing of opposites and synthesis, but its transformation into human knowledge obeys a dialectical process. Human beings see and understand the world through their stream of consciousness and symbolic interpretations of it.

Since the only way that an individual can know an object is through an act of recognition, rediscovering in his own self-consciousness complementary images and words, consciousness can only recognize itself in an other—an other of desire. This other is the object of will that consciousness desires in a negative relation, because it can only apprehend it as an image and an abstraction. Consciousness, then, becomes self-consciousness, discovering that the desired object is not outside of itself but rather within as a mental representation.[6] Consciousness is obliged to transit through the other in order to return to itself in the form of the other. In this sense, consciousness can say "I" only in relation to an other who serves as support for the process of recognition in a dialectic situation.

The Mirror Experiments

We ought now to examine the famous mirror experiments of Henri Wallon, who used Hegel's dialectical basis of "knowing" to construct a psychology or "science of the human" in the late 1920s and 1930s. Wallon's ideas were grounded in a dualism that focused on the development of the mental life of the individual in a cultural environment. Using sociological, psychological, and biological factors, he sought to understand human beings as animals who responded to genetic predispositions, acquiring language and speech as their bodies developed complex and mature nervous systems. Through interactions with others, an experimenter could determine what part the social factor played in the normal development of the individual. For Wallon, these dialectical transformations of the physical, mental, and social psychology of humans began in early infancy and childhood. A succession of "discontinuous stages," continually restructured in crises brought on by physical, social, and mental development, were the key to the transition from childhood to adulthood. Wallon saw psychology as a dialectical transition between two situations. For him, the actual events in an individual's life were secondary, as were conditioning factors and constitutional fixities. He was suspicious of the notion of the Freudian unconscious as an uncontrollable force moving between biology and psychology; his own psychobiology is essentially a "theory of mentalities" focusing on the culture and heredity of individuals as two primary areas requiring study and concern. Finally, Wallon was interested in an interdisciplinary approach to the mental development of human beings, criticizing Freud's excessive use of symbolism and considering psychoanalysis more of a philosophy than a science.

In 1931, Wallon's report on his mirror experiments amazed and excited the French world of science. These experiments sought to explore infants' first encounters with a mirror and ideas about themselves and their bodies that developed from these experiences.[7]

Wallon's experiments with animals and their reflected images seemed to begin like a fairy tale or dream. Stories of animals and infants who saw themselves in the looking glass and reacted with joy or repugnance at what they beheld filled his notebooks. In his laboratory, Wallon discovered that if he removed a drake from the presence of his female and placed him in a chamber lined with mirrors, he misrecognized his own image for that of his mate. In a similar experiment, a dog's reaction was one of avoidance even as he accepted affection from the experimenter; he shunned his own reflection, turning his face away from it. A monkey showed himself to be both clever and stupid in the same experiment. He attempted to reach his hand behind the mirror, but when he discovered nothing there, he became as angry and agitated as an enraged beast.

Wallon then compared the reactions of children with those of his animals, noting different responses according to the age of the infant. Until the end of the third month, the infant seemed unaware and insensitive to his image in the mirror, but then changes in his reactions did occur. His eyes began to fix themselves on his reflected image as though it were an other with whom he could interact. The beginning of a smile seemed to appear, although the researcher could not be sure that this was recognition of some sort or gas. Two months later, the infant smiled at his own image in the mirror and that of his father when the two were next to each other. But when his father spoke, he turned his head toward where the sound was coming from in surprise. He had not yet learned to differentiate between the reflective image and the actual presence of the other in time and space. He did, however, know that there was a relationship between the person's presence and his reflection in the mirror, but he could not grasp the cause-and-effect relationship between them. He seemed willing to attribute to each of these images an independent reality, separate and apart from one another.

At the tenth month, further changes were noted. The child reached out toward his image and looked at it if his name was called out by the experimenter. He perceived the self outside of himself as a complement to his natural self. To unify himself with this perceived other self, the child has to accept a dual necessity; first, he must accept the mirror image as one that exists even though it possesses only the appearance of reality; and second, he must attest to the reality of an existence that escapes direct perception. He then has to deal with the contradictions these insights represent. He encounters sensory images and representations that are not real and real images "unavailable to sensory apprehension." He must learn to transform immediate experiences into reflective thought, making distinctions and equivalences that sharpen his awareness of himself and others in his environment. His ideas about his own body, which are essential for normal development of his self and ego, are shaped during this period. At first, no relation is established in the mind of the infant between the image in the mirror and the real image; later, a relationship develops, allowing him to constitute himself as a unified individual. These stages are the prelude to the third stage—that of symbolic development and language, which will allow the child to begin to organize his sensory experiences into an intelligible system and world. For Wallon, one year is the age when a threshold is passed in the child's ability to structure and receive symbolic messages. In another experiment, an attractive girl was put in front of a mirror. She began to admire the hat she was wearing on her head; the images in the mirror were helping orient her gestures toward her body and clothing. This ability to distinguish between her images in different spatial locations defined the symbolic function, allowing the child to begin to differentiate between subjective and objective reality. This girl was not satisfied with establishing a relationship between the image in the mirror and herself. She recognized, accepted, and separated the reflection from the actual person, understanding that the image was subordinate to the real person standing before the mirror.

At fifteen months, the mirror experiments showed new insights on the part of the infant. Asked to point to his mother, a child first pointed to the mirror image, then turned to his mother, smiling. He had mastered the duality of the image, which is not real, and that which is real and causes the mirror image to appear in the first place. He understood the unreal and symbolic character of the mirror image.

Wallon believed that the individual went through natural stages or transformations. These contained a symbolic and imaginary dialectic that helped him resolve the many contradictions, disputes, and conflicts of social and mental life. In this, he viewed consciousness in much the same way as Hegel had done, unifying philosophical, biological, and psychological concepts. His experiments showed the transition from the mirror image to the imaginary, and from the imaginary to the symbolic. In 1938, Jacques Lacan used Wallon's theory to strengthen his own Oedipus complex theory. It seemed to allow for the individual to project himself into a mirror image, to construct a form of himself as an imaginary ego controlled by a narcissistic structure. But Lacan described these processes from the perspective of the unconscious rather than from Wallon's vantage point of consciousness: the specular world in which the primordial identity of the ego is expressed did not contain any others. All this was couched in a negativity, in a need for recognition—the "presence-absence" of an other or of others. Relying on Hegel, Lacan asserted that the person who did not struggle for recognition outside his family circle could not achieve his personality before his death.[8]

In *La vie Mentale*, Lacan synthesized much of Wallon's work, reinterpreting it from a Freudian perspective with terms steeped in Hegelian philosophy. Family complexes, according to Lacan's theory of psychoses and personality, lie at the heart of the formation of human identity. That personality is structured in a purely negative manner, through a series of unconscious representations or images that define an identificatory modality of recognition or misrecognition, seemed evident from the ways in which language structured and interpreted the social world for the individual.

In the beginning, there is a "weening complex" that is characteristic of the newborn and early infant, a primal need of "parasitism" that leaves a deep and lasting impression on its psyche. This remains as a residue, an oceanic feeling described in Freud's work on religions as the ultimate mass illusion. In a second phase, the "mirror stage" of Wallon's experiments becomes apparent. This follows the end of the weening period and permits the child to achieve reflective or "anticipatory unity with the ego, in which the 'other' or 'others' have no place." In a final stage, the other appears as a player in a familial struggle for recognition. It is at that moment that the Oedipus complex Freud described so poignantly begins.

The unsophisticated judgment of an individual who has become conscious of a thought assumes that his awareness of it is being received without interference or mediation. The great anthropologists[9] have given expression to the individual's tendency to turn every experience and thought into language. Through speech, these experiences of the thinker are made personal and intelligible; they become part of his symbolic and imaginary world, fitting into an order and sense that only language can provide. This world is the world of the unconscious, the world of the Other, and it is important in developing a person's identity and sense of reality. But even his perception of reality is steeped in misrecognition, since the average person believes that he is experiencing the world directly as it is, that there is a one-to-one correlation between the world and his ability to know it. Hegel and Kojeve have shown that what we see are only images, images that are inside our head and distorted by limited views and understandings and our tendency to change everything into words.

Now the world makes sense for the individual. Now it has a beginning and an end. Now it has meaning that can be explained by dialectical thinking. Now the vast universe, which cannot be seen or understood, can be conceptualized in ways that make him think he grasps the reality around him. The symbolic structures the imaginary and the real, providing ready-made, rational structures, even though the world is not ready-made or rational. It provides an orderly environment for people in a world of colliding planetoids and exploding stars; it gives men and women the rules and rituals they need to make sense of their lives on Earth.

The Structuralist Perspective

Structural linguists have already given us insights into the ways that individuals mistakenly see themselves as the source and certifier of meaning and consciousness. The subject is viewed as a prisoner in a world of consciousness and symbols, a world that appears all around him but is, in fact, within. Sensory perceptions are shown to be mere images dominated and transformed by words and linguistic categories. The individual senses the world around him, perceiving it through his stream of self-consciousness. He is the center of this world, and nothing happens there unless he senses it in some way. Images bombard him in a never-ending succession. Only when he focuses on a particular object does it take on meaning for him. Then it seems to zoom into his consciousness, producing an image he often mistakes for the thing itself. The outside world is understood in the context of a symbolic and imaginary order that harmonizes everything of which he becomes aware.

Much of this discussion is based on the ideas of Ferdinand de Saussure and Roman Jakobson who we have written about elsewhere.[10] A linguistic sign, in their view, was divided into two parts—the signifier and the signified. The word or sign that signified something in the world was an arbitrary one that had little or nothing to do with the object itself. Another person understood what was being said because he shared a common linguistic heritage with the speaker. The words themselves did not identify objects in the world outside of these mutually agreed upon and understood conventions. Thus, an automobile, as an example, was not identified by any innate characteristic of the automobile itself nor by the speaker who used the word. The object's identity was communicated to the other through a system of language dialectics that depended upon the similarities and dissimilarities embedded in the structure of the language being spoken. The speaker did not endow the automobile with the meanings we normally associate with such an object; these were determined by the word that had been designated arbitrarily by the language of the speaker and his listener.

The distinction between speech and language is also an important one. A word can only send a message if it does so within the structure and signs that are a part of the language being used. The spoken words of individuals, then, can never be an expression of inner reality or a unique understanding of the world. No matter what his message, no matter what his intentions, the subject who speaks must use the language he holds in common with the Other. He must make certain his words conform to the demands of a structured, dialectical sign system.

Another concern of structural linguists was the nature and development of language systems and especially the concepts of *langue* over *parole*. Langue looks and sounds like the word language and can be loosely translated as a linguistic system conveying a set of grammatical structures that support an individual's actual speech. Parole, on the other hand, applies to the behavior of speakers and listeners and what is actually said in a particular situation. It focuses on the words that are chosen, with important consequences. The structure of the entire language determines the position and meaning of every other part of it, including the words that are chosen in a particular communication. Changing the meaning of one group of words alters every other feature of what is being transmitted or signified to the Other. The totality of language has priority; the words are chosen from a language to which everyone has access, but they are spoken in an individualistic way by people interacting in personal encounters.

So the structures of languages ought not to be sought in any empirical study of their current or past usages. Rather, the researcher needs to become conversant with psychoanalytic theory, looking for what lies beneath the linguistic structures and messages of speakers. What is seen and heard by individuals when they venture into the world is not the grammar and syntax of communication systems but their effects. These are the state and social apparatuses that carry on the development of Otherness in the individual, teaching him to understand and accept the language, culture, and economic system he inherited. The structure of his language is unconscious and invisible to all but the trained observer. Yet every member of the social system can apply these grammatical and phonological rules without thinking about them—that is, unconsciously. This ability to use universalistic signifiers in speech is a genetic heritage of human beings and allows the social world to exist and reproduce itself. The number of languages spoken on the planet is incredibly large, yet certain immutable elements reappear in all of them.

According to Saussure's theories, the speaker who uses the acoustic image of a sign is the signifier, or the subject who initiates speech. He uses a linguistic sign to communicate his thoughts and intentions to an Other. This sign or word has a value because of its dialectical relation to the many other signifiers present in the common language of the speaker and his listener. Its meaning is deduced when the listener coordinates that which has been signified with the acoustic signifier or word. Saussure placed the signified object or thought above the signifier, separating them with a bar that indicated the moment when signification or understanding occurred. The words chosen to signify a concept had many meanings in the language system of the two persons speaking to one another. But in their particular situation or relationship, they took on personal and intimate meanings or nuances. Later, Jacques Lacan was to take this neat linguistic model and turn it on its head. He placed the signifier first, or above the signified, which had a primordial position in the communication processes. The word itself had no immediate meaning but became an important determinant for the unconscious of the speaker. The speaker himself was controlled by the unconscious and acted as its agent, dividing the self into an imaginary ego and a powerful id.

This new model explains the individual's uneasy condition. He is represented by a signifier or word that is nothing more than a linguistic symbol of the unconscious. He is not in control as Saussure would have it; he is controlled by the id. This means that he becomes the divided one, who is represented by a series of words, a chain of signifiers in which the messages spoken are not congruent with his utterances themselves. He becomes an object in a symbolic order, who, for another signifier, is represented in an unbroken chain of signifiers. In this sense, individuals are defined by words in the form of a language speaking in their stead. Lacan rephrased René Descartes's cogito from "I think" to a more Freudian "it—or the id—speaks." Whereas Descartes had said, "I think, therefore I am," Lacan replied, "I think where I am not, and where I am, I do not think."

Descartes stressed the consciousness of the individual, while Lacan emphasized the Freudian unconscious, the true master in the mind of humans. Descartes's work viewed the individual as someone who could reflect upon his consciousness, who could repress and call to consciousness certain thoughts and feelings. But he did not take into consideration the ways that the unconscious affected language. Interestingly, Freud himself remained in the Cartesian tradition even as he provided Lacan with the insights that led to its supersession by the decentered individual in structuralist theory. The subject was now seen as someone who knew not what he was; he was a subject divided and controlled by the unconscious and by language.

Yet this approach to the study of consciousness has certain limitations. There is a de-emphasis on history, with little or no attention paid to the changes occurring in language systems over time. The structures themselves are seen as givens that human beings have inherited and have been unable to change since the first communications many centuries ago. For structuralists, the modifications of languages in the past have not diminished their timeless qualities and syntaxes. They isolate language from its users, ignoring the social, economic, and cultural practices within which languages were formed and refined. Structural linguists seek to move beyond such rationalistic and historical analyses to the laws that govern all language systems wherever they have developed. Naturally this is merely a sketch of structuralist orientations. The concepts cover a wide variety of thought, and structuralism ought to be seen as an umbrella term. Here it is meant to convey another idea that preceded Lacan's construction of a decentered, language-defined inner identity and core.

Claude Levi-Strauss used Saussure's thoughts about signs and significations to explain the social practices of kinship, economic systems, food, and myth. He explained these social practices as communications that were also constructed within the rules of linguistic structures. He thus found a way of describing such structures as part of an unconsciousness that was transmitted through language, showing their unity even as they remained separate and apart from other cultures. Each system was related or derived from an earlier one, and all existed primarily in the symbolic world of significations. By paying close attention to the structures behind these significations, Levi-Strauss believed a universal language of the mind could be uncovered. Again, the individual was seen as a subject whose consciousness was illusory. Beyond language or significations, he had no ready access to social reality or intercourse. His cognition was language bound and further distorted by ideology and limited horizons. Levi-Strauss saw in myths the cement and cohesiveness of societies, whereby individuals were tied together by their common adherence to the signs and linguistic representations of their common social heritages.

The Symbolic Order

What are the origins of our thoughts? How do we come to see ourselves and others around us? And can these thoughts escape the influences of our parents and earliest experiences? The question can be raised whether there are any ideas that are original and unrelated to those espoused in the homes, schools, churches, and state agencies of modern society. We shall therefore leave open the possibility of such phenomena while insisting that generally such ideas violate the laws of psychic determinism upon which psychoanalysis is founded. The child in our previous examples will find himself forced to take his place in the symbolic order created before he was born.

No one has emphasized more sharply than Jacques Lacan the diffuseness of these concepts once they leave the precise world of language and enter into the world of the mind.[11] In Lacan's work, the symbolic order refers primarily to the language of the individual's familial experiences. He suspected that the communications from outside sources were of less psychological significance, even though they later played an important social or socializing role. For Lacan, the symbolic order was evidence of the unconscious as it developed its identity as the discourse of the Other, teaching the child how to communicate with the nurturing Other while locating himself in the family structure.

It is quite clear that Lacan's confusing use of the concept of the unconscious had its roots in Freud's shifting metapsychological theories. In an effort to simplify, we may say that Freud saw the unconscious as a biological part of the psyche, classifying it in an early period as a feature of the human being's instinctual apparatus where memories were stored or repressed.[12] These memories contained the collective unconsciousness and memories of a family and people, including primal repressions that were beyond the awareness of the subject's consciousness. Freud used the unconscious in other ways as well. It was a way of identifying everything that was not in the consciousness of a person, or in his preconsciousness; it was, in short, not a biological but a psychic phenomena. Lacan incorporated both the biological and the psychic ideas of the unconscious into his own thinking, adding a special emphasis to its linguistic essence and structure. For Lacan, an individual's use of language was an unconscious process in which he attempted to communicate with another unconscious listener. This was done by using the common signification system or language open to them both—the language they had inherited from their parents.

It is worth explaining again Lacan's use of the term "Other," for in his early years of socialization and adjustment, the child learns to desire what the Other desires. He learns to internalize the discourse of this important Other, who is usually the parent in the first instance. (In other situations, the term will come to mean an awareness of Otherness, or an identification of those others who are objects of his thought and communication.) Sometimes the Other was used by Lacan to refer to the subject's parents, as we have shown in an earlier section. Yet it was never to be understood as another person. Rather, it was seen as another way of referring to the Freudian unconscious, although for Lacan, this unconscious now became the place where the common language and culture of the Other was located. Otherness is important for the individual because it helps him to understand the imaginary relationships he has with those around him: he views them as objects of his own desires who are also other subjects. But in reality, these others have been categorized as linguistic entities; they have become objects who can be talked about and placed in the symbolic order that labels and controls the lives of humans. The others in the subject's life cannot be thought about without referring to the language that structures and organizes them into a social totality, without referring to the locus of language, or the Other. The Other, or the unconscious in this line of thought, is the Other for the person who wishes to communicate. It creates an intersubjective world that allows the subject to speak and be understood through an unconscious process of speech and language. The unconscious has a dialectical relationship with the unconscious of others; it can only communicate when the meaning of its meaning is received by another. As the location where the universal code or language of communicators resides, the unconscious, or Other, is not inside the psyche of the speaker or listener. It is in a third position, providing both the sender and receiver with a common signification code that they can use with one another. All attempts at discourse involve individuals in the process of coding and decoding messages. This is done in an unconscious manner by both speakers and listeners. Both need to communicate in order to gain the recognition that is so vital to their own sense of connection and well-being in the world. The speaker must concern himself with this Other if he is to get his message across, if he is to speak in a way that will elicit an appropriate or hoped for response. Yet he is limited in what he can say by the common language and culture he shares with the Other. Also, he has little or no control over the way his messages will be received.

Not even the deepest, most closely held secret thoughts of a person can escape this unconscious reference to an Other, or Otherness, since they, too, must be transposed into words before they can be used in a meaningful way. To repeat, the unconscious and the Other are concepts outside the individual for Lacan; they are transsubjective in nature and steeped in language and third entities whenever dual discourses occur. For Levi-Strauss, the unconscious is seen as an intrapsychic rather than a psychic phenomena—a function of the social world's collective consciousness. It is this collective consciousness that creates and maintains the world in which humans live, establishing a symbolic order that gives it rationality and meaning.

Thus, children learn to desire what the Other desires; they feel needs intensely and are completely egotistical, internalizing the discourse of the Other voraciously.[13] But soon they become aware of Otherness and new identifications and objects of thought and communication. And it is natural that this should be so, for we expect that the child, as he matures, will awaken to new situations and people. It is true that the Other initially refers to the individual's parents. Lacan uses it as another way of speaking of the Freudian unconscious, that place where the Other is located. Otherness is important because it helps children understand the imaginary relationships that individuals have with one another: they view each other as objects that have been objectified by linguistic structures. Thus, Others are not active subjects; they are objects that can be labeled and discussed without their knowledge or consent. The unconscious, then, is the Other for the person who wishes to speak, creating in that moment when he is understood an intersubjective world. The unconscious has a dialectical relationship with the unconscious of others in the communication process. It can only communicate when the meaning of its meaning is received, decoded, and understood by an other. The unconscious is the place where the code of language resides. But again, it is not inside the body of either individual; it is in a third position between them, providing the sender or signifier with a plausible receiver. All attempts at human discourse involve these processes of coding and decoding linguistic messages. They are done by the unconscious without awareness or conscious thought. The need to communicate is a primeval one, tracing itself to the earliest moments of life when the neonate must either receive recognition of its demands or perish. He must concern himself with the Other from the first if he is to make himself known, if he is to have the food, warmth, and attention that he needs to live. What a person can say to another is limited by their common language and culture. Yet the newborn has no control over the way his first demands for recognition are received by the Other. Not even when the child learns to speak at a later age can he escape the symbolic order imposed on him by his family and class.

Others have written that repression is not possible unless it is considered part of an interpersonal world.[14] Lacan echoed this idea in his *Discours,* defining the unconscious as transindividual. The signifier and his listener need a common code or language that they can interpret and understand. It is in this sense that the unconscious is seen as a language and the locus of the Word. Lacan's more precise definition of the Other is that of the site of the signifier or Word, the place from whence the collective unconscious dominates and makes possible the world of humans. The medium of that discourse is the language (and culture) people share with one another. The unconscious is not only the repository of an objectively agreed upon symbolic order and code, however, but also the repository of familial, social, and personal myths and histories. In it is found the hostilities common to ethnic groups and social classes and the illusions and identities that owe their continued life to the collective consciousness transmitted through language. Racial and cultural memories are embedded in the language of peoples. Through their transmissions, individuals come into contact with what Freud called the collective nature of the unconscious. The symbolic order operates in the realm of the Other, the place where language is held in common. In Lacan's lexicon, the Other and the unconscious appear to be synonymous, describing both the condition of others and the collective unconscious they share. The idea that the unconscious is "the locus of the signifier"[15] indicates that these vocalizations are a part of a chain of phonetic utterances, another level of the unconscious that provides individuals with insight into the kinship structures of the symbolic order.

The symbolic order, then, thinks predominantly in language, creating and sustaining the imaginary world of humans. Levi-Strauss showed that no person can act in a symbolic way alone; an Other, another's unconscious, must be present before that can happen. Even when an individual is thinking to himself, the Other is present, mediating his thoughts through the use of language. And in familial and educational settings, there are always others who come forward to play the role of the Other. Thus, a child's first experiences with kinship structures are a continuing discourse or dialogue with an increasing number of Others who share his linguistic and cultural heritage. The communication between teachers and students, as another example, is also a symbolic one, grounded in the mores and moral understandings of the moment, with one unconscious seeking to discover what the other demands of it. This leads to inferences and translations that allow both teachers and students to understand what is being communicated in the classroom setting.

To summarize, the transformation of ideas into language is the primary method through which the symbolic order establishes its rules and regulations. Language constructs a situation that establishes the symbolic relationships into which a child is born, determining his race, religion, class, and so on. It is the instrument that children use to learn about the world as it is, conforming by desiring what the Other desires. Finally, it is the order that demands conformance, no matter how much the individual's fantasies and animalism rebel against the imposed order.

The family is the first and most important feature of the symbolic order, giving the newborn a sense of the mother, father, siblings, and so on. It integrates the infant into a daily routine and teaches it the myths and world view of its past. This world of symbolic relationships and structures is defined by linguistic signifiers, chains of words that have their roots and meanings steeped in other signifiers that came before them. Thus, symbolic relations are governed by signifiers that describe the otherness of the world in an orderly, rational way. The rules of the family lead to the laws of human society. These determine how civilized persons will live together, spelling out in some detail what they may and may not do.

Through language, the self creates a consciousness that others can understand and identify. This identification exists at the moment an individual presents himself to others and is part of a universal consciousness that develops between them. The self learns to separate itself from itself, from the primal roots from which it originated. It becomes a social object that others can speak about and reflect on, and the struggle between civilization and its discontents, which Freud wrote about so eloquently, comes into focus. In the symbolic order, the individual fuses himself to the language and culture of his group, learning to see himself and his consciousness through them. Language becomes the mediating force between a person's recognition of his conscious self and the independent recognition by others. On an everyday level of understanding or common sense, the individual seems to be a subject who speaks. But Lacan has shown that speech and language are unconscious processes, and that language speaks and humans merely listen. Language makes individuals into signs, reducing them to objects that can then be placed in the social, cultural, and symbolic orders and in the transsubjective world of others. It is the link between the individual psychology of subjects and the kinship structures within which they live their lives.

3

Language and Kinship Structures

After primal man learned that he could improve his condition by working and hunting in larger groups, it became a matter of some importance that he learn to communicate with clansmen. Others became important to him, and he used signs and simple significations to inform them of his needs and desires. Language began to structure his relations with kinfolk and enemies, securing him from the dangers of the natural world. Claude Levi-Strauss has sketched the fundamental role of the symbolic order in these processes, citing them as the foundation of man's first elementary kinship structures.[1]

Even earlier, he may have learned the ways of his own flesh and blood, fitting into rudimentary nuclear structures. Following the great anthropologists, we can suppose that these first families of men, women, and children were connected to one another through a web of affiliations that defined social structures and sexual practices. There were variations, of course. The time spent developing these rituals and traditions was limited by economic needs and privations. Nevertheless, primeval man must have thought about them: Who or what was the female? What role did she play in the emerging structures of the clan? Perhaps primal man believed that he knew the answers to these questions, but there were unexplained emotions that accompanied the sexual coercion of women in the primeval family. He could not fail to recognize his own arbitrary and all-powerful position, even as he wished for more voluntary, consensual relations with family members. He may have refused to recognize his own role in their subjugation, preferring to use women as he wished. Or his reactions could have sown the seeds for more loving relationships characterized by later kinship structures. Still, a certain physical force was needed if he was to maintain his leadership and control over his family. Here the role of language provided tradition-based rituals that he could use for such purposes. For Freud, the moment when the sons overpowered the primal father was a crucial one in the development of modern civilization. Yet the totemic restrictions they later placed on one another required phonological laws that allowed them to speak and make themselves understood to one another. These first restrictions and taboos were the beginning of human civilization, the moment when "laws" and "rights" were first given voice. The life of primeval kinship groups was now founded upon communal work and the force of love as it developed between men and their sexual objects—women. The most important immediate result of language's ability to impose order and control over human affairs was felt in man's increasing mastery and power over his natural world. And since this made him better equipped to live in stable communities, he was also able to work and hunt in ever larger numbers, further increasing his control over his environment.

This recognition of the crucial role of language needs elaboration. Memories of primal man were stored in his preconscious or unconscious, suggesting a collective past important enough to be preserved. Many of these remembrances could not easily be recalled. Yet the unconscious was more than a mere repository for past myths and unremembered experiences. It was the locus of man's emerging language and symbolic order, the place where structural laws delimiting the impulses, images, and memories of clan members were stored. The Other, in these first movements toward humanness, was the place where the unconscious, accumulated vocabulary, language, and culture resided. These articulated the personal history of the clan and its members; their significance derived from the organization of symbols according to the rules and regulations of Otherness and the totems and taboos of a people. Discourse became more complicated: without the linguistic structures they developed, the words primeval men spoke would have lost much of their meaning.

The memories that founded these first kinship structures continued to operate as myths and traditions, growing out of transmissions from mother to child. This created a world of ever-changing personal discourses and exchanges, but the unconscious structures governing these discourses and exchanges remained the same, reproducing the symbolic functions and order of family and kinship life.

The laws of symbolic functioning were few in number, but they made it possible for clan members to recognize one another and act accordingly. They bound together first the immediate family, then the clan, and later whole regions of people in ways that were much more intensive than was possible through common work interests alone. Word presentations now signified relationships; these brought with them duties as well as gratifications, and the world took on a concreteness that it did not possess earlier. The chains of signifiers gave words a specificity they could not have in isolation and made for a more complex family life.

Freud felt that the use of the word "love," as one example, was deliberately careless and genetic. It was used to describe the relationship between men and women who were sexually drawn to one another, leading them to marriage and family duties, but it was also used to express the feelings between parents and children, and between siblings. These relationships were seen as love with an inhibited aim; they constituted sensual love that had been prohibited by the group even though they continued to exist in people's unconscious. Both types of love reached outward, extending new bonds of affection and friendship to people who had been strangers in the past. Men and women who loved each other in a sensual way led to the formation of new families through marriage ceremonies, while aim-inhibited love produced friendships that had value in their lack of exclusivity. The taboos that individuals placed on love were severe, and they may be said to have ushered in the human era.

This can be seen most easily in the prohibition against incest, the harshest restriction ever placed on the erotic tendencies of men. The reasons for it have been widely reported in anthropological and psychoanalytic literature. The taboo expressed itself as a conflict between the demands of the individual and those of the emerging kinship structures that wished to bring ever-larger groups of people together. But the nuclear family tended to exclusiveness, often cutting itself off from others and making it more difficult for members to become part of a larger circle of life. To move away from the family became a task for every man and woman, marking the moment when they entered adulthood. Primitive society helped by providing a symbolic world of myths and rituals wherein their experiences were related to those of others who had lived before them.

Furthermore, the guilt experienced by the murdering brothers laid the foundations for human culture. Prohibitions against incest represent the interests of group life above those of the individual and are tied to the laws of kinship structures. These interests obliged a family to part with one of its members to strengthen community ties, strengthening also the group's ability to live in greater security and abundance. From these totems and taboos, it was possible for men to formulate marriage rules as systems of exchange that were recorded in the language as socially sanctioned laws and communications.

An aside seems in order. Levi-Strauss came to see Freud's theories of the origin of myths and taboos as misplaced.[2] The prohibition against incest, in his view, dealt with modern unconscious desires and not with those of primeval man. These modern unconscious desires needed to be kept under control. The manner in which Freud thought we expressed regret for our lost opportunities of incest were, according to Levi-Strauss, an expression of a desire to resist the order of modern civilization.

This may well be true. But most anthropologists agree that with the acquisition of speech and language, man crossed the threshold of nature and entered the world of civilization and culture. It was not only his sense of the clan. Totems and taboos demanded sexual and social sacrifices for both the good of the clan and his own good as well. Words gave rise to other words that identified members and came to be recognized by the individual as code word substitutes. Thus, we can assume that in earliest times, human beings were defined by words that they later came to see as their essential being or essence.

For Levi-Strauss, kinship structures in primitive societies correlated with phonemic structures of language. He wrote that the act of giving is more important than the gift itself, since these exchanges are the glue that holds clans together, even in modern times. It is in the act of speaking and listening that important commitments are made in marriage rituals, even when the words themselves seem uninformative or redundant. And these verbal exchanges were the world into which newlywed members and their children entered, once the rituals and laws had been codified into language and folklore. Men and women were now married in ceremonies, and the woman was seen as the one who was given by another family; her sisters would be given in the future when they reached maturity. These rules of living together were enmeshed in gift-giving rituals that unified families and clans. The marriage ceremony became the moment when the exchange occurred, according to the laws or rules of society as they were understood and transmitted by elders. Here the past history of a family or clan was repeated in the individual's thoughts as they were passed on by the language of significant others.

The tendency on the part of human beings to restrict sexual life to expand social and cultural units was bolstered by the symbolic pact that took place when a man and woman married. Taboos, laws, and traditions imposed unconscious structures that propagated and shaped the destinies of every family member. The love a woman gave her husband was now seen as something that transcended her spouse. The sacred love that bound her to him was directed toward all men and toward their duties to their families and clans. Conversely, through the taking of a wife, the man swore fidelity to all women, and to the new family members of his clan. The husband and wife became the embodiment of universal types or symbols in the exclusive marriage contract. They were defined by language and the Word and were the essence of the human couple.

Human kinship structures were made possible by these feelings of guilt, these renunciations of sexual gratifications. The life of primeval man was one of extreme egoism, aggression, and instinctual gratification with language playing little, if any, role. The structure of human civilization began when man passed from animalism and nature into the symbolic order and culture, when he accepted the prohibition against incest and established rules for marriage exchanges. The sense of guilt, whatever its origins, helped men to unify themselves into larger social units.

Furthermore, language soon came into prominence and displayed its organizing and ordering tendencies—words that signified objects in the world tended to provide men with a false sense of knowing and security. Words represented the interests of the social groups that developed during these first moments of civilization. When primeval man made a sign or phonetic utterance that was understood by an Other, a unity occurred between them and between the sign and the object itself. The concept of danger that primeval man might want to convey to an Other was transformed into an acoustical sound, taking its place in the mind of the Other and alerting him to the impending danger. For example, the concept of cave and the word "cave" were now equated in the minds of both the speaker and his receiver. What Ferdinand de Saussure has called an acoustic image of "cave" became part of the language, signifying the concept "cave" and the ideas and sensory images the word implied.

"Cave" was the signified object, the concept of the cave and not the cave as it existed in men's external reality. Confusing the two would certainly lead to serious injury and death, and primeval man seldom made such an error in his thinking. The urgency in the expression of the word alerted the Other to the fact that danger was at hand, either before them or in the cave itself. Depending on the situation, the spoken word could mean "Get to the cave, there's danger!" or "There's danger in the cave!" or "I can't wait to get back to the cave!" and so on. The signifier's relation to the reality it sought to convey was transformed by action words and situations that provided the word "cave" with different significations or meanings.

The tendency to mistake the words and symbols for the objects themselves could exist in man's thought and behavior. The word concept conjured up the appropriate images and ideas in his head, giving him a concrete sense of the real world in which he was living. Danger could become an important and all-embracing word for the clan living in caves. Yet these linguistic signs were arbitrary ones that were accepted by members over time; they had little relationship to the object or the sounds such objects might make. Caves could have been called something else without affecting in the least the comprehension of Others, if members agreed to it.

Thus, the symbolic order or function allowed primeval man to objectify his thoughts and actions by putting them into words. This permitted him to control his environment more securely and to hunt in well-coordinated packs. It enabled him to warn others and to be warned when danger approached him or his family. As a member of a larger hunting group, he could rank himself against other members and against others in the clan. When a dangerous hunt was called, it was natural for him to volunteer as a hunter, for that was the word used to designate his identity. He was a member of a culture, a collective effort of the clan to bring nature and the needs of humans into a more orderly relationship. The work of the culture was to convince members that sacrifices were needed for the sake of the common good, confronting them with dire consequences if they chose to go their individual ways. Since a man does not give up his sexual pleasures easily, he had to be forced to accept the taboos and ritual laws binding him to his clan. Men were seen as destructive animals with antisocial and anticultural tendencies, who had to be controlled by the group.

The inevitability of death forced prehistoric men to think about existence and the meaning of their lives. These first thoughts may have been primitive and naturalistic, but they did bring the questions of life and death into sharper focus. Laws and rituals were enacted to honor the dead and to prepare them for their lives in the next world. However, not all primitive civilizations did this. The economic and social structures of a society influenced the amount of time its people spent thinking about these cosmic problems. Nevertheless, primeval man must have asked himself more than once: "Who or what am I? Why am I here?" Perhaps primal man felt that he knew the answer to these questions, but there were mysteries that accompanied the death of a loved one that must have deeply troubled and confused him. He could not fail to recognize his own fate in those of others who had died before him, even though he may have turned his face away from them. He may have refused to recognize his own mortality, choosing to deny the fate of all creatures. Or his reactions may have bordered on disavowal or rejection. Still, a certain sense of denial was necessary if he was to survive in the harsh climate of prehistoric times. Here, as we have already shown, the symbolic order was providing an ordered and orderly world that he could use for his own purposes. In this respect, civilization requires language if it is to provide its members with an understandable world. Sacrifice of the rights of the individual forces society to develop ever stricter rituals and laws to govern how individuals may act toward one another. A cultural community must have a common language to bind it together, to provide it with sacrifices that integrate families, so that larger and larger social units can unify themselves for common interests and concerns.

Primitive societies provided important transition rituals for children who were moving into puberty and adulthood, using ceremonies sanctified in signs, words, and gestures. At an early age, boys would accompany men on their less dangerous hunting and fishing expeditions, thus preparing them for the tasks and skills they would need in manhood. The extending nature of the clan and tribe meant that older folk now had a hand in socializing the young, and that members had an opportunity to observe relatives and friends in different stages of their life cycles.

Some tribes used ritualistic language to emphasize sexual pleasures and the freedom of their youth to experiment; others stressed reproduction and discouraged children from sexual pleasures of any kind.[3] Tribes encouraged their members to live, play, and work with age mates; this helped when members were forced to take on new responsibilities demanded by initiations into secret societies.

In return for the individual's sacrifice to the group's welfare, tribes offered gifts and honors; as punishment, recalcitrant members were often physically abused or cast out of the tribe. Primitive societies existed to assure members a minimal level of food, shelter, and clothing in a harsh and unrelenting world.[4] The flow of goods and people was in the form of barter, serving as an outlet for binding discourse and the development of personal and familial relations. And all of this was part of the symbolic order that the tribe imposed on its members through language and thought. These exchanges recognized the existence of certain economic and social relations between individuals and groups. Actual gifts or exchanges were almost beside the point, however; mutual recognition and reaffirmation of relationships were what bound individuals to the clan or tribe. And these were accomplished in a world described and made sensible by the ordering propensities of language.

Puberty was dramatized by linguistic recognition—an individual had reached the age of sexual maturity. The transition was dramatized in dances, rituals, and words that attended to the individual's passage from a dependent position to one of economic and social responsibility. Language thus assisted in the physical and socioeconomic maturity of a tribe member, helping him through this difficult, transitional period. His new status was authenticated by magic and religious sacraments, and these relied upon signifiers and signs that attested to this new status in the group. The importance of these rituals can be seen in their existence in tribes and clans from food gatherers to fishing and hunting peoples. They were what made man into a human animal, capable of entering into an ideological order structured in language and speech.[5] Special symbolisms in action and words represented the cycles of birth and death that so dominated the culture of primitive tribes and clans. Thoughts and religious ideas were transmitted to individuals from elders, and these became the structure and foundations for tribal understandings and actions. Men of action digested these symbolic mysteries and accepted them as definitions of themselves and the lives they led.

Rituals made it possible for members to believe in and understand the world as they found it. Anthropologists studying present-day primitives recognize in them all of the emotional attitudes of modern man. The primitives show fear in some situations, love and hate in others, and grief when tragedy strikes them or one of their fellow members. The rituals and symbolic understandings allow them to attribute guilt feelings to others who were outside the community or godlike in nature. Primitive societies are mired in custom, and custom and tradition help them to deal with human problems that develop during the life cycles of individuals. Certain words and phrases provide emotional solace to those who are bereaved, and these are often said in public and treated as parts of the tribal rituals. The boundaries between the imaginary and the real world are more often fused than separated, as are the inner world of the self and the outer world of the community.[6]

The Ancient Israelite Confederacy

Insight into how these kinship structures evolved in later, historical periods can be gained from a study of the ancient Israelite confederacy.[7] A child born into this tribal association was a member of an extended family and tribe bound together by common worship and ritualistic practice. There were other tribes, of course, but there was no single civil, judicial, or administrative body to bind them together. Wars and internal disputes were frequent, and unity forged only when an outside threat endangered all of the tribes. Every tribe used a common language that made it possible for them to share ideas about God and culture.

In peacetime, disputes were settled by men who were prophets. They were war or religious leaders who decided what was to be done, but their power was limited by religious, military, and political forces in the confederation. Cohesion was based on religious beliefs and the idea of a common stock of people. Most of the tribes were stock breeders, justifying their customs and moral values by referring to the traditions and practices of their ancestors. Social solidarity was based on religious commingling; extended families were able to come together in their worship of God.[8]

Children underwent rituals and were taught the story of Moses and the covenant that was made between the Lord—Yahwe—and the children of Israel. The liberation-from-bondage story was told each year, along with the miracles that ended in the destruction of the Egyptian armies in the Red Sea. These miracles were portrayed as a sign of God's power on Earth. Yahwe was seen as all-powerful and his promises dependable; Israel was in His lasting debt. These ideas were not much different from other religions of the region. But the religion of the ancient Israelites was founded on this covenant or pledge that Yahwe had given to his people. He swore to favor Israel above all others on the condition that she worship him as the one and only Lord of Hosts.

A bilateral agreement was ratified in language and passed on from one generation to the next. Israel, and Yahwe, were united in a covenant sealed in words, and this established unity among the various tribes of the confederation. The demands of the confederacy now had both a sacred and a secular sanction, and those who ignored its demands defied the Lord of Hosts. Language was used to pass on the word, and the word included Yahwe's promises and Israel's responsibilities to Him.

At first, Yahwe's words were probably part of an oral tradition.[9] But later they were written down. Yahwe was a god of war who could not be crossed. He rewarded his believers but demanded the blood of disbelievers and enemies. The plagues that He visited upon Egypt were remembered at the Passover seders that were held in every Israelite home.

Still, this God who could cause all sorts of natural disasters could also be beneficent toward believers. He sanctified the laws and customs of the confederacy but made allowances for new revelations and changes in the ancient covenants. The religious commandments had the force of myths and taboos, forbidding adultery and incest, and opening the way to marriage exchanges that bound the tribes into larger units.

The tribes also provided ritual and religious explanations for the life and death of its members.[10] Each was linked to his family and ancestors by the commandments that were written into the covenant with Yahwe. Death was not followed by another life in the hereafter, but a sinful life was sure to shame the descendants of the deceased sinner. The worship of Yahwe was the authority that shaped tradition and communal laws, leading the way to a just and honorable life. These laws were written down on tablets and later in the Old Testament. They made plain the duties that ancient Israelites were bound to obey while hinting at God's terrible punishment if they were disobeyed.

The Israelites validated the laws of their society by anchoring them in the covenant with Yahwe. The prohibition against incest and adultery were two of the most important commandments because of their role in preserving the identity of a man's family and tribe. Scribes carefully documented the lineage of families, and biblical writings described instances in which God had become angry because of man's transgressions. The problems associated with the familial complexes were managed by age-group segregation and rituals that culminated in the bar mitzvah at thirteen years of age. The dramas of the Oedipus complex were seen as events that had taken place in the past and that had to be reconciled before the young could marry and establish their own families. Myths helped to assuage the anxiety and guilt of children, assuring them that their feelings and desires were natural and a consequence of their age and dependent status in the family.[11]

The mores and taboos of kinship structures contained preferences, commands, and prohibitions related to the sexual and economic behavior of individuals. These symbolic structures were incredibly involved and complex, with a nomenclature rooted in the dialectics of language and its presumptions of causal effects and totality. The symbolic order always revealed itself to humans as a closed system, a unified whole or universe in itself in which everything was explained and understood. Often, it appeared to be indistinct from the world it symbolized and completed, but it was always part of the unconscious processes that made human communication possible.

Kinship Structures and the Unconscious

In venturing more deeply into kinship structures, we must review the nature and role of unconsciousness. Elements of this process can be discerned from the unconscious nature of speech and language. That the concept of a cave is not the cave itself has been discussed in our review of Hegel and Lacan. Words are merely an arbitrary symbol for the thing or place we wish to designate. As Lacan put it, the world of words creates the world of things. The things themselves are merely images entering our stream of consciousness in a confused and often troubling procession. But we have also seen that words and the rules of language bring a certain order and concreteness to our fleeting, ever-changing environment.

In addition, we have found that men and women can speak to one another because of the symbolic order that language creates for them. The communications are made easier when both have a common frame of reference and culture. The fact that speech and language are unconscious processes has affected the way that humans have conducted themselves in the past. Even today, the rules governing exchanges of women are tied to custom, tradition, religious beliefs, and the state. Gifts are one way that recognition is given to the new family, tying both spouses more securely to the older families from which they originated. Marriage ties, which have been commonly ordained in sacred and secular law, have retained language and the Word to structure the lives of young people for the benefit of the group. Such laws provide unconscious structures and a world of symbolism that harken back to other times and places. It is in these kinship structures that the Oedipus complex appears again and again, marking the fantasies and boundaries of family life in the emergent years of human development. The man who later marries carries with him these unconscious understandings of marriage rituals and structures. In accepting and verifying the symbols of the ceremony, he swears, in effect, to give up any incestuous feelings he may have harbored or will harbor in the future.

Human sexuality is now governed by primordial laws that provide marriage partners with a way of behaving toward one another. A culture of the many asserts itself by placing regulations and demands, and marriage partners are constrained from copulating with other men or women. Mothers, fathers, and siblings, too, are forbidden as sexual objects.

The fact that such laws are enforced by kinship structures is accepted without much thought; for it is no more than a way of accepting the traditional beliefs and behaviors that have been passed on by our parents. Yet traditional laws and beliefs find expression and legitimacy in the structure and order that language imposes upon them. Without thoughts and language to support it, true kinship would disappear, and the order, preferences, and taboos binding families together would be impossible. Symbolic identification provided primitive man with beliefs that tied him to his ancestors and to the group, as it does for modern man today.

Freud found that the father was the figure of the law, the person who supported the symbolic function as it emerged in human families. This produced words that sustained the ideas and beliefs by which the tribes lived. Words gave men and women the names and relationships that governed understandings and actions, providing them with a valid basis for including or excluding individuals from their group.

A symbolic, imaginary order takes the place of the real world; it is so pervasive in the lives of humans that it envelops them in dialectical networks before they are born, as was shown earlier. Those who are to be parents talk about their children and give them names and social identities before they are born. The parameters of possibilities in life are given to them by chains of signifiers, identifying who they will be when they are finally born. The words that will describe them as a doctor or a janitor, a Jew or a Christian, a black man or a white man, already exist, even if they are not spoken by family members. Even in death, these words follow individuals, deciding where and when they will be buried and whether or not they were good or faithless persons.

The cycles of language provide men and women with a sense of family and security until the more confusing teenage years intervene. But always, the stream of words emanating from the unconscious shapes struggles for recognition in the symbolic order of the families and neighborhoods. The Word attempts to make itself understood and recognized, allowing individuals to transfer previous understandings and insights to new encounters and experiences. It makes an object of others and helps individuals to see the world in a dialectical manner that has its rationale in the linguistic structures governing human speech.

Kinship structures assign cultural spaces to members, and these often reflect their duties in the family or clan. The Word exists in a concrete discourse that gives rationality and meaning to the individual's consciousness, even when the world itself seems to possess few of these qualities. These discourses, in turn, are grounded in the traditions, cultural mores, and natural functions that contribute to the health and well-being of the group. The role and status of individual members become a chain of signifiers belonging to a signified social order.

We have tried to follow the work of Levi-Strauss and others, but we have been forced to make our own interpretations in view of Lacan—namely, that the unconscious is the locus of language, imposing form and structure on the world of humans. The point is that the unconscious always refers to collective memories and myths, effecting a sense of continuity in human affairs by relating the individual and others to a symbolic order. It establishes cause and effect and a collective tradition that binds people to one another and causes humans to think in terms of beginnings and endings.

We have thus been able to find a place for the unconscious that is more Lacanian than Freudian. It is no longer to be seen as a depository for individual fantasies and repressions alone; it is no longer the psychic locus of the irreplaceable human person. It is now the third entity from whence the symbolic order emanates, providing humans with unique insights and understandings of the world. And it is accessible to all men and women who live within the same language structures and laws, the same culture. What is more, this third entity can be reduced to the totality of the laws of human conduct governing individuals in a particular social system.

The unconscious imposes regulatory laws on those who use its linguistic and cultural signifiers, forcing them to suppose a world of logic and order, since these seem meaningful in the context of the structures and syntaxes of languages. Unexplained forces and heavenly motions must be explained; they must have a reason. Emotions, memories, and impulses likewise need to be ordered and subordinated to needs and desires as they are expressed in the symbolic order. All the attributes that we prize in thinking are to be found in these unconscious, symbolic functions. It is there that the individual learns the words that describe and give meaning to his own life and to his relations with others. Yet signifiers take on more personalized meanings when they become part of a discourse that is shaped and shapes the structures and laws of unconscious processes. The word "authority" means one thing in the family setting, another thing at work or in school, and still a third thing when it is used in a theoretical discussion or in organizational structures. The images and words of a tribe or clan create myths and understandings of the world, much as they do in today's highly impersonal, industrialized societies. They are the materials that develop from individual and collective discourses and memories, gaining their structures and meanings from their relevance to symbolic functions and ongoing interactions. The language used in these discourses has a very small number of laws and phonemes that individuals can employ to make themselves understood.

To sum up, we describe the words and discourses of humans as unconscious processes that structure social mores and understandings. We believe that it is reasonable to assume that these define social conventions such as marriage ties and family life, providing them with a concreteness and structure they would not ordinarily possess. Communication mediates between the sexes and between individuals. Becoming conscious is connected with the application of words to images and thoughts, making the bride and groom understand the significance of various rituals and customs. The first stirrings of symbolic thought must have transformed women, as one example, into things that could be exchanged like designated objects. Yet men and women were always more than the sign that represented them; they were always human beings who could listen and speak as Others. In marriage ceremonies, each person retained his or her individuality while assuming new roles and responsibilities common to his or her people's culture. Beyond the words that signified them, the couple often had value for one another that transcended the signs defining them in the symbolic order.

Let us add that the individual's psychology has always been subordinated to the social demands of his culture. Certain roles had to be assumed if reproductive processes were to be accomplished; certain other roles had to insure that the tribe or clan was able to feed, clothe, and shelter its members. These roles were reflected in the relationship of a series of signifiers, thus fixing persons in a web of symbolic affiliations. They were unconscious structures, much like the speech and language that described them. They assured that in the world of humans, the primacy of language in interpreting reality would provide an order that fixed members in their assigned places.

Other things should be mentioned at this point. The particular language and cultural system of an individual completely encapsulates him, making it impossible for him to step outside of it; he cannot become a dispassionate observer, no matter how much he might wish to do so. He cannot escape the distortions and structures that symbolic functions impose on his perceptions and thoughts. Following Levi-Strauss, we can assume a moment in human history when men split themselves off from the animal kingdom and the natural world while maintaining many of their previous characteristics and behaviors. This separation from the animal world occurred when man moved beyond his needs and desires to a new plateau—that of communicating with others of his species about his needs, desires, and fundamental anxieties. There must have been a moment in time when language came together, ending the long period of sign systems and gestures. At that instant, man became aware of the world in which he lived as a transitory figure. He did not know the world any better as a result of his new capabilities, but he sensed a new unity and order, a new ability to amass, name, remember, and relate things to each other. The signs and gestures of the past contained little or no relationship to one another. But with the advent of the symbolic function, man's knowledge of the world became more comprehensive and continuous. Now the things that were signified and the signifiers themselves had a unity and complementary nature. They permitted him to establish and ascertain relationships as they evolved in personal encounters and in retained memories. And they all had their origins in the unconscious, or the Other, and its ability to give man a sense of the Otherness that was all around him.

From this point onward, man's train of thought signified his world as a totality he could know through thought and discourse. He now had concepts and words he could use to understand the world in which he lived. The intensities of these ideas allowed him to separate his universe according to the structures and limitations of symbolic thought, forcing signifiers and the signified into relationships that led to congruence and comprehension. But a third entity was always needed if the unconscious nature of speech and language were to be understood and translated into an intersubjective phenomena. The Other became a transindividual entity not controlled by the speaker's consciousness. He was only aware of his spoken words after they were uttered; he knew not how they were selected and related to other signifiers that had come before them. The unconscious appeared as an element in his personal reality, revealing itself in memories that were recovered; it was the place where drives and impulses were stored or repressed. But this unconscious was also the primary instrument of human thought and ideation, the locus of language and the precondition of meaningful speech and discourse. The speaker, who unconsciously sent messages, and his receiver, made sense of word presentations by relating them to other signifiers and to ongoing situations.

Human discourse had a certain autonomy grounded in the seemingly contradictory idea of unconscious thought. The unconscious was a blank space or falsehood for Lacan; it was "the censored chapter." But these censored thoughts and ideas could be retrieved or identified by relics or markers. Their inscriptions were to be found in the structure of language and in the childhood memories of patients. The way that a person spoke, his vocabulary and his style of life and character, were clues to the unconscious, as were traditions and legends he accepted as his history.

For Lacan, the unconscious was the subject's personal history. It was a series of happenings that had, at certain key moments in life, turned him in certain directions. These occurrences were the forgotten moments of shame and humiliation that accompanied the harsh socialization processes of his earliest years. But they were remembered and relived in symbols and psychic tensions that appeared to trap and obsess the subject. These early experiences of childhood were replete with victories and defeats associated with the training of one's bowels and imaginary erotic fantasies. Different stages of development existed when they were experienced in childhood and later remembered and spoken about in adulthood.

Collectivities and Consciousness

If we return to the ideas of Levi-Strauss, it becomes clear that for him the elementary structures of kinship have great variability. Such structures are needed if the social order is to reproduce itself, preparing the young for the responsibilities of adulthood.

But they can include family structures or not, depending on the customs and culture of the tribe. They do not possess a "natural" mode of relating to the neonate or to the other members, yet they do have linguistic functions that instruct others to do so. Incest was not viewed as the ultimate taboo until men began to use language, until they lived in the symbolic order. There is no biological reason why incest should be proscribed in the life of the family, but there are good economic ones. When hunters gave way to food gatherers and stock herders, civilization became more populous and complex. It was now necessary for larger tribes to live together in harmony; the incest taboo and the exchange of women in marriage were inaugurated as ways of unifying different familial and tribal members. Even earlier, the symbolic functions had forced human conduct to see itself, increasingly, as part of a larger purpose or universe. These functions became paramount in ordering and explaining natural catastrophes and events that accompanied the normal life of individuals and tribes. The human order was one of meaning, a symbolic world that possessed a universal character. In it, all experiences were understood and explained by strings of signifiers; the individual was seen as a meaningful actor who could influence his own fate and the will of the gods.

Thus, the symbolic function orders and constitutes the human condition and defines kinship structures. Preferred behavior and prohibitions are indicated by it; commands and status systems evolve from its words. And the ever-increasing complexity of social structures asserts itself and is made conscious through language's labeling of individuals and their relationships to one another. The universe of the human is organized around dialectical insights emanating from the symbolic nature of language itself. These hold it together and give human life its meaning, order, and intelligibility.

Does all this mean that the collective unconscious, for which Freud was so severely chastised, exists? Or are the individual and collective unconscious the same thing, as has been suggested by others? For Lacan, the symbolic order functioned continuously from birth, enveloping humans so completely that they were unable to escape its hidden presumptions, designations, and rationales. What we perceive in life therefore is much more influenced by the symbolic function than we realize. Life is viewed as an orderly flow from birth to death, with ritual points that commemorate puberty and adulthood. Again, language completely defines and transforms human experiences, lifting them out of the natural order and into a more imaginary, symbolic one.

The symbolic order, then, provides the central structure for man's experiences in the world and for his imaginary powers. All of his abilities to think about this planet, this universe, this economic system, make use of these symbolic functions and the relations they establish. Even the fundamental anxiety provoked by death becomes the subject of the imaginary function in this symbolic order, giving his existence meanings that go beyond his perceptions and reason.

How, then, are we to understand this process further? Are all human thoughts a consequence of the Word, as the Bible indicates? There is no doubt that the world a neonate enters already exists. Name the important persons in his family—mother, father, sister, brother—and slowly he learns to say them and understand their meanings for him. These people have specific functions in his life and in the maintenance of family structures and relationships on which he depends. The prohibition against incest is also a given in this world, instructing family members not to sexually desire their parents and siblings, while implying that sisters will be given to strangers in marital exchanges in the future. Thus, the rules of marriage and extended kinship are codified into words that govern the imaginary, symbolic world of families. A sister will be a wife to another, someday, and the woman in her own house. In this sense, the relations between people are understood as part of the laws of the tribe or culture, ordering and regulating the ways they respond to one another and forcing incestual impulses into repression.

So we must ask again: Is there a collective unconsciousness as Freud and others have implied? Our answer must be "no"; there is no common spirit or soul that unites the newborn with the dead. There is, however, the symbolic order, which passes on the myths and memories of the past through the unconscious medium of the Other, the unconscious. This thirdness functions in our thoughts and choice of expressive signifiers, and is also the atmosphere in which we live and communicate in the world of humans.

The Other contains the idea of Otherness within it; it is the world of significant others that must be considered and understood before symbolic functions can exist. The individual is shaped by Otherness and comes to recognize his personality in the language others use to describe him. Otherness represents interhuman discourse and contains within it the unconscious structures and memories of an individual's past history. Every attempt at speech presupposes the existence of an intelligent listener who can hear and respond. A teacher tells a student to sit down, or a priest signals the moment for prayers; the chain of signifiers is directed toward a significant other and makes him aware of the mores and moral understandings of the moment. These spoken words are always addressed to others, even when we think to ourselves. It is through the constant stream of signifiers that humans learn the myths and histories that tell them who they are, where they come from, what loyalties they must affirm, what memories are important, and what beliefs they must harbor about sexual practices and death.

The Other, then, can be understood as the unconscious, or the awareness of Otherness, or a third element standing between individuals who wish to communicate. It is the locus of the Word, the linguistic heritage that exists among people, providing them with a common language that they can use both to speak and to listen. The words of the family reflect the attitudes and beliefs of kinship structures. It is in the first communications that the child starts to learn about the universe and his place in it; it is then that he begins his initiation into the religious rituals and beliefs that will bind him to his family and people. This will be followed by a long apprenticeship. In modern society, schools will teach him to take his place in the social and economic hierarchy of the nation; they will also teach him that the order of things is natural and unchangeable. Everywhere he turns he will hear the language of his culture, maturing finally and taking his place as a citizen and worker in that culture and system.

4

Reproduction

The division of society into economic superstructures is a fundamental premise of Marxian theory; this alone makes it possible for us to understand the persistence of social, economic, and cultural formations and to discover how they reproduce the conditions of present-day life. To put it in more functionalist terms, the current economic and cultural formations cannot survive without replacing the instruments and conditions of their existence. They are obliged to reproduce the labor power of each generation and to secure the relationships in which production and the distribution of wealth take place.

For traditional Marxists, the material means for reproducing the labor power of capitalism is purchased by the workers themselves as they consume commodities. This is not a biological concept for Marxism but rather a part of the economic relations that develop in market economies. But reproduction of labor power is a complicated task, requiring that the new work force be indoctrinated with appropriate ideological attitudes and dispositions.

Consciousness of the habits and skills of a particular position can be learned on the job.[1] Experience shows that this is an effective way to condition the behavior and attitudes of the new worker, teaching him to see things as older workers have seen them in the past. Yet a state of consciousness that accepts the conditions of modern capitalist production requires more. A long training period in which the individual is immersed in language and the symbolic order is required if the habits and skills of modern production are to be inculcated in him, if he is to accept ideological and economic subjugation in the workplace. These processes cannot be explained by economic considerations alone—we know that thanks to the work of Louis Althusser[2] and his collaborators. We can say that both the skills and attitudes of new workers and their willingness to accept the economic system as a given are secured by extra-economic practices and institutions. (Or, if we carry the traditional base-superstructure theory further, by the state's interventionist character and its tendencies to act as an agency of class domination.)

The state (and its power) has been the focus of the class struggle during the past century and a half, and its repressive apparatuses have been seen as agencies representing the interests and concerns of capitalist classes. But many would undoubtedly object to these simplistic descriptions. "No," they might say, "modern capitalist systems have parliaments and congresses and rest on the consent of the subordinate classes they govern; so long as citizens accept and consent to the existing economic relationships and their assigned places in them, physical force is not needed." To disagree with such a statement, or to point to the prisons and large-standing armies of modern states, would be futile, especially since repressive state apparatuses of overt repression have been largely replaced by a more sophisticated means of ideological and cultural inculcation.

Ideological dominance of the ruling classes in modern capitalism is secured through definite institutional forms and practices; these are the ideological state apparatuses of the ever-expanding capitalist entity.[3] Antonio Gramsci found that very powerful cultural and linguistic ideas existed and were passed on to youth in schools; churches; families; communications media; literary, cultural, and sporting organizations; trade unions; and political parties of modern social systems. These noneconomic structures functioned within a symbolic world of language and signs, achieving through ideological effects and intimate social relationships an acceptance of the status quo. They seemed to operate apart from the repressive state apparatuses that secured by force the exploitive relationships of capitalist systems, providing a shield behind which ideological state apparatuses functioned.

Thus, we obtain our concept of the ideological state apparatuses from Gramsci and Althusser. These play a major part in the reproduction of the relations of production, inculcating skills, attitudes, and aptitudes that serve the dominant classes. Such insights support Althusser's central hypothesis that under capitalism, the school and the family have become the most important of the ideological state apparatuses. The church and family couple, which secured a continuity of productive and social relations in feudal society, have now been replaced by more secular institutions.

The concept of reproduction caused Althusser to revamp his base-superstructure theory, using Lacanian psychoanalytic ideas to explain socialization processes that assure the continuity of capitalist systems. The unconscious acquisition of language and a sense of Otherness are important mechanisms in these ideological state apparatuses, allowing the reproductive requirements of capitalist systems to be internalized in the social and psychological world of individual actors. But, we may ask, is there really an absolute separation between state apparatuses that are coercive and those that rely on ideology and other forms of persuasion? We know that families and schools have their own forms of physical punishment, and armies and nations often call for allegiances based on ideological and patriotic slogans. But the problem is one of degree, according to Althusser; a distinction can be made between those state apparatuses in which force or ideology predominate. Gramsci suggests that the methods of class domination are combinations of these consensual and coercive practices and are inseparable in their occurrences in families and schools.

We must also note that Althusser's ideological state apparatuses include widely divergent social institutions that are joined for purely empirical reasons—that is, for their social functionality. Families and churches, to name two such apparatuses, seem more private than state institutions, even though they are linked to state power, but Althusser uses a functionalist criteria to justify his treating them as noneconomic structures contributing to the reproductive processes.

For us, however, the view that these are noneconomic structures needs to be challenged. We recognize that much of their activities transcend economics, yet they are involved in producing replacement workers; they expend labor power in order to create productive value at a later date.

Ideology in Action

It will be seen on further consideration that what we call ideology is not that different from notions of symbolic and imaginary orders. It is all of one piece to us, for individuals must always translate images and ideas into language before they can become real for them. So let us look at some of the ways that scholars have defined the concept of ideology in more recent times. Althusser attempted to define ideology in more precise terms, seeking to free scientific discourse from its effects. For him, the differences between ideology and science were ones of cognition: ideologies were unaware of the suppositions supporting their arguments, and science was not. Ideologies were not cognizant of their problematic aspects and were not conscious of their theoretical assumptions.

This dichotomy seems easy enough to disprove. Both ideological and scientific discourse make use of speech and language. Both exist in the symbolic and imaginary world, choosing to know the real within the dialectical structures and limitations of language. Both assume a meaning and a rationale to human existence, even though the world is unknowable to them. True, science does make an attempt to understand its theoretical orientations, but this is done imperfectly, at best. It is impossible for humans to escape the ideas of creation, order, and totality built into the very foundations of linguistic structures. And science has seldom been noted for its awareness of its own suppositions. Indeed, science may require a suspension of critical attention in such matters. Even mathematics has certain assumptions that must be accepted without question by its practitioners. And, of course, that logical, closed system is another triumph of the symbolic and imaginary function. Thus, we may speak of ideologies and science as two ways of thinking that try to illuminate the world so as to make life more intelligible for humans.

Nevertheless, some writers have differentiated ideology from science by examining their structural characteristics. Both contain apparent truths that can be verified after a fashion. But ideology seeks to be more practical than science, pretending to inform us on matters of theology, morals, education, and politics. Ideologies are the ideas people live by in daily life; their power and life span depend on helping individuals to make sense of their lives. Science, on the other hand, does not tell us how to live. But its ideas do make their way into other areas of consciousness, changing our views of god, man, and country.

So far we have been rather vague in defining the concept of ideology. It is time now to consider the work of Raymond Guess,[4] who divided the term into three categories or meanings. The first definition of the term "ideology" was a descriptive one: ideologies were made up of the beliefs and folklore kinship groups passed on to their children. They were transmitted through language and contained the myths, religious understandings, and political wisdom of a people. So long as men lived together, they were in need of ideas that explained their experiences (and deaths) in a meaningful way. Ideologies were belief systems that explained human life: there was a beginning and an ending, there was an orderliness and a plan, there were morals and values, there were births and deaths, friends and enemies, and so on. All civilizations have developed symbolic and imaginary orders that have explained the creation and orderliness of the universe and the meaning of life here and in the hereafter.

The second usage of the term "ideology" was the Marxian one: ideologies were delusions distorting men's relations with one another and keeping them in subservient and oppressed positions. So long as men did not recognize and exorcise them, they were condemned to live a life without consciousness. Ideologies were doctrines validating the existing inequities in society, assuring the dominant classes that their positions and oppressive practices would prevail.

A final, positive definition of ideology was that such thinking was needed in all civilized systems and had to be created again and again. New leaders needed to provide followers with updated understandings of their conditions and responsibilities. They needed to provide a set of beliefs and attitudes that were not specific to those of a particular class but of the entire group or nation. And they had to be appropriate to changing needs and times.

It is essential to abandon the overly negative understandings of ideology before we can form any correct view of its origin and value for human cultures. In Althusser's view, ideological orientations are a fact of social life, something that societies do wherever they are formed in human experience. They were (and are) a system of concepts and beliefs that command the attention and allegiance of a class or people. They have their own structure and logic, using symbolic functions to provide adherents with common understandings of their historical roles in society. The symbolic and imaginary orders provide identities and a world in which individuals can understand one another, make sense of their lives. Over time, ideologies become systematized beliefs that serve to reproduce the way things are in an existing society; they are the method through which the labor power of capitalist societies are reproduced in the families, schools, churches, media, and so on. Working- and middle-class families convey ideological understandings to children, who internalize them without much thought or conflict. Each individual develops his own sense of himself and his primary group through language; we call this his cultural, sexual, racial, and class identities in bourgeois society. His sense of the Other and of Otherness creates an illusionary world of symbols in which he learns to see himself as someone possessing free choice, someone living in a social system governed, in part, by his consent. It is these mental images and understandings of the real world that are the site of the cultural class struggle for neo–Marxists, even as the mirror effect and the development of the voice of the Other create the conditions for homeostasis in capitalist systems.

Ideologies do not explain reality as the sciences do. Rather, they are part of ongoing relationships and realities; they are part of the world humans must adapt to before they can be considered fully human. They are common-sense understandings that people embrace as they struggle to survive in a senseless and unknowable world, often accepting appearances for essences.[5]

There is little question that ideologies are an outgrowth of human thought and language, two unconscious processes that typify the human condition. Ideologies are simply the way in which people think and express themselves. Althusser asserts that they are not specific expressions of dominant or subordinate classes, although they may reflect such interests. Human beings seem to need these ideological structures as much as they need social and economic order. Within ideologies are the ordinary person's understanding and beliefs about himself and the history of his people. These are transferred through speech and language, forcing men and women to take positions in the symbolic and imaginary orders, which are suffused with ideologies. Societies without ideologies are unknown to us and must be classified as utopian visions. Ideologies cannot be replaced by science or rational thinking because science, too, must use speech and language. And in these usages of unconscious linguistic structures ideological effects are certain to make their appearances. Ideologies are the means through which people experience the world and their relationships to one another. Only through a determined search for the unconscious structures supporting such ideas can human beings learn to understand why they exist and why they are needed.

So we may ask: What basic human needs does ideology fulfill? For one thing, it places people at the center of their lives where they appear to be subjects who can act independently. It also plays an important role in the reproduction of the social order and the labor power of capitalist systems, teaching the young to recognize the Other and Otherness as natural, unchangeable givens in their lives. Ideology is conveyed through unconscious processes, providing itself with normative values that influence the way that people live their lives. These structural Marxist ideas are at odds with Marx's view that ideology was a delusional form of thought filled with falsehoods and needing exposure. We agree with his formulation but insist that if we were to unmask old ideologies, new ones would pop up in their place. The strength and duration of ideologies were most recently reaffirmed in the defunct Soviet Union and Yugoslavia, where long-dormant cultures and beliefs were resurrected after almost one hundred years of repression.

On further consideration, we must tell ourselves that ideology is connected quite firmly to class interests as well. For it is that consciousness that inculcates the values and beliefs of the family through the medium of Otherness. But ideologies tend to support and subvert the status quo in society even as they form a collective consciousness that allows people from different classes to struggle with one another.

We are tempted to assert that ideology is like the unconscious, both suffused with the dialectical structures and limitations of speech and language. But an end to ideology would require an end to the symbolic and imaginary orders, thus ending also human life as it now exists. Ideologies unite men and women in families, clans, and classes, forging them into social institutions and systems. Even in a classless society, they would be needed in order to produce and reproduce the bonds between children and parents, as a first instance.

Questions now arise. Can ideologies distort reality and hide the oppression of the weak in capitalist systems? Can they hide the power that supports certain legal and social formations in modern society? A quick answer seems to be "yes." But these distortions have more to do with the symbolic function and its imaginary propensities when confronted with the unknowable features of human life. They appear to answer fundamental questions associated with death and resurrection, and relations in the workplace. In this symbolic and imaginary world where everything makes sense and has its own name and place, the world is an orderly, cohesive whole, providing men and women with reasonable amounts of safety and control.

This does not mean, however, that we believe that the ruling classes do not have ideologies that they use to dominate others. Ideologies are the unconscious myths that people live out. They are genetically acquired and passed on through the unconscious mediums of speech and language. If human beings are to subordinate their impulses and needs, ideologies will be required to persuade them. It is probably impossible for people to live without myths and illusions, for these are given with their mother's milk and reinforced by the symbolic order. The end of ideology would be the beginning of a new ideology that explained what life was all about in the "post-delusional period."

Why, we may wonder, must people live like this? Why must they be condemned to a world of distortions and oppression?

Why can't they understand the actual conditions under which they live and work? The answer seems to be that rational thought has been unable to produce ideas and beliefs that can assuage men's fears of vulnerability and death. It has been unable to clarify the ways in which speech and language distort the real, forcing men and women into symbolic and imaginary worlds of the mind. Also, ideology teaches people how to act and react, making them more valuable to society and more pliant in the workplace.

Ideological State Apparatuses

Now that definitions of ideology have been established, a further discussion of ideological state apparatuses seems in order. These agencies are responsible for preparing youth for their roles in the social and productive sectors of society. They must do this and more: these apparatuses must provide individuals with ideological effects that support their claims to legal-rational authority and control. They must talk about freedom and choice even as they limit both. The cultural class struggle goes on in these apparatuses, where the language and tradition of the educated classes are internalized. Youth are forced to recognize, over time, the distance that separates them from the arbitrary language and culture of the educated classes.

But the school and family, to name again the two most important apparatuses, are dominant in the reproduction of the labor power of capitalist systems. The efforts of teachers and parents appear as altruistic labor at first glance, as noneconomic behaviors serving the interests of the economic base of society. Yet they also have the effect of propagating the mores, laws, history, and moral understandings of the status quo. The family is often thought of as a private sanctuary, not a state apparatus. However, state policy and legislation influence and regulate marriages and family life even as they pretend to avoid doing so. The struggles over abortion rights or the right of gay people to marry are examples of state intervention; another is the public-school system that forces youth to attend schools that stratify them and the knowledge they are taught.

The reader may exclaim at this juncture that these reproductive schemes have an economistic bias to them! Capitalist systems, in particular, seldom set up quotas or requirements for families and schools, and the needs of the economy seem to shift with each new technological advance. But families and schools must first reproduce their own social relations before they can perform ideological functions for the economy and the state. Also, social reproduction is never a neat process. The ideas of state institutions are often challenged by those who are suffering, and by those whose religious or political beliefs differ from those of established authorities.

But what are we to make of the idea of ideological class struggles that are so important to neo-Marxists? How are they waged by those who are in the working and middle classes? How are ideologies used to transform the consciousness of people living in the advanced capitalist systems? And are they universal phenomena existing in every society, functioning as the social cement that holds people together? Certainly our description of the effects of the symbolic order on thought and perception would answer these questions in the affirmative. Still, these ideological beliefs constitute a distortion of social reality, blinding people to the realities of the social and economic system in which they live.

Ideology, Praxis, and Power

Althusserian theory has directed our attention too much to the separateness of ideological thought.[6] We can learn more about ideological class struggles if we maintain the classical Marxian view that ideologies are inseparable from material struggles in capitalist society. Until now, the only guide we have had is that ideologies mask the social relations of power in families, schools, and workplaces. But how is this possible, the reader may ask? How can we deny the separate characteristics of family and class ideologies? What does it mean when we say that ideologies teach us how we should live our lives? How can they do that?

We know the perspective from which we should answer these questions. Ideology is the way that human beings think about the world; it is an outgrowth of their daily lives in families, churches, schools, and workplaces. These state apparatuses depend on ideology to sustain relationships and practices, and these reinforce ideological understandings about life and work. When ideologies change, they do so because situations of power have changed. Marx insisted that ideology was not to be separated from the social relationships forced upon people in the productive sector. The relationship of his parents to the productive sector shaped every aspect of a child's existence, determining where he lived, how good his prenatal experience was, the amount and quality of time his parents could spend with him, the speech and language he was taught, the kind of school he attended, and so on. The question, "How are ideologies formed?" can be stated: "How do people think about their lives?" And the answer should be: Through the words parental and educational structures use to describe their identities and places in the social hierarchy.

These word presentations are unconscious communications that help a child to make sense of himself and his world; they provide limits and Otherness, teaching him how he is to act and what he can expect in neighborhood schools and elsewhere. But these ideological constructs have the net effect of disguising deeper social and economic struggles that cause him and his family to live and work as they do. Even a critique or an unmasking of them will not cause them to disappear. Even an understanding of why they exist may not raise significantly consciousness of individuals. The economic and social conditions calling forth these ideological definitions will still exist, demanding new rationales and explanations. People will need ideologies that they can lean on and live by in their daily lives.

Every attempt to solve the problem of schooling in capitalist society has had to deal with its ideological content. All have tried to learn how educational systems reproduce their own social relations and those of the workplace. We are not alone when we say that the primary purpose of schooling is inculcation.[7] Nor will we surprise the reader when we introduce the concept of ideology in its Marxist context: schooling performs its ideological functions by deception, or what Pierre Bourdieu has labelled symbolic violence. It is by hiding the relationship between educational practices and the social structures of capitalist systems that it pursues its functions of inculcation and reproduction.

We are thus forced to conclude that schools are not neutral in the ideological and class struggle occurring in mass society. Their apparent autonomy is seen as a sham when we examine the history of schools and their relationship to the state. Schools make an important contribution to society by reproducing the status quo both in its intellectual and cultural variants. Still, they have been able to maintain the fiction of neutrality and autonomy, providing significant ideological services to capitalist society. The culture of the school is transmitted through pedagogic practices validated by the political power of the state. These practices, in combination, provide students with a language that defines them and their place in the social system.

The relative autonomy of schools has been presented as a given that must not be questioned, even when society is changing drastically, and industry and commerce are in a state of ferment. Or, more properly, schools must be seen as neutral agencies in the class war, whose teaching staffs consist of benevolent individuals concerned only with helping children. This ideological understanding has been used to legitimate the internal practices and traditions of schooling itself, making educational systems extremely difficult to reform. Teachers have become more professionalized civil servants in recent years, but their methods of teaching have remained arbitrary and authoritarian. This is because schools have always been tied to other agencies of capitalism, even as they denied such links; they have arisen from the social and political customs and from the functional needs and beliefs of those who funded them. But in pursuing their own purposes, they have developed a special history and practice, borrowing methods from mental hospitals, military and penal institutions, and the charity schools of the early nineteenth century. Educational systems have paid lip service to the ideals of the larger society while trying to insulate themselves from the special interest groups around it, pointing to their professional ethos and tradition. The division of state schools into grades, career teachers, examinations, and graduation degrees cannot be understood unless we know something about the immigrant experiences of the last century and the reforms that established our current bureaucratic system. These bureaucratic structures have persisted even as the world has moved into the postindustrial period because of an inertia specific to state schools. The organization of educational systems seems to be opposed to change of any kind, insisting on a return to basics and a simpler past. Yet, through all this resistance to change, the educational systems have managed to pass on to each generation of students the business culture and ideology.

The first thing that becomes clear to anyone who examines the results of ten or twelve years of schooling in the United States is the ideological effect: schools produce workers (and citizens) who have internalized the ideas of capitalist economics. They have been trained in a culture that encourages them to think, perceive, and act as compliant workers, accepting things as they find them. Teachers, too, suffer from the need of schooling to standardize pedagogic messages, persevering through years of meaningless education. This prepares them for their roles as inculcators; later, student-teaching experiences assure that their apprenticeship will have the intended effect. They will be unprepared to teach in large, unruly classrooms, and will, in desperation, teach as they were taught many years ago. The self-perpetuation of pedagogic practices is essential if schools are to maintain their authority to reinterpret the social, political, and economic demands of society while maintaining the integrity of their organizations.

How, then, can we best study educational systems in capitalist society? There is little doubt that we must study them historically, showing their links to the economy and other state ideological apparatuses. Their essential functions of inculcation and social control can then be revealed. This should be done within a sociocultural perspective, and the relations between educational systems and other state and economic institutions should be made clear.[8] The study should include the class relationships that predominate in a particular school or district, so that the hidden power of the state can be made explicit.

The unquestionable finding remains, however, that the formation of state schools is based on religious and cultural foundations as well. How does this affect the primary function of schooling? When we recall that the school, family, and church are three of the most important agencies of reproduction in mass society, we may conclude that there is more to schooling than mere civil and economic reproduction of workers. This view is a tenable one. But our focus remains on the family and schools, two of the three most conservative institutions in society. Both use symbolic actions and pedagogies to teach youth of the world as it exists or has existed in the past; both conceal the dominant forces behind their inculcation activities. Emile Durkheim believed that the role of every educational system was to conserve the values, mores, moral understandings, and culture of the past. Schooling performs this task of conservation through daily pedagogic action and work, maintaining the symbolic order as an unchallengeable given. When things are going well, the symbolic order created by pedagogic work reinforces the status quo and is accepted with little thought. Educators focus on traditional practices, reproducing their own organizational structures and those of the workplace. Schooling seems obsessed with its need to perpetuate itself, using grading, grades, directive instruction, and other features of authoritarianism as traditional aspects of modern pedagogy.

Thus, schools appear as a neutral agency, concealing their contributions to the class and cultural divisions of society. In this guise, they are better able to defend and conserve the status quo. They succeed by obscuring the inculcation function and its effects on the class identities of students. The language and culture of a student does not change in schools. Over time, it becomes a signpost, a way that others recognize a youngster's class position and possibilities in mass society.

Teachers wrap themselves in a righteous, normative order; they act as a moral authority who seeks to legitimate their right to monopolize pedagogic work. They present themselves as separate and apart from the state that hires them, appearing to owe little to any forces outside their classrooms. They work for altruistic reasons and for the good of the children they serve, upholding the rights of Americans to equal opportunity and access. These are important parts of their ideology that blur their relations with the state and class structures of capitalism.

Schoolteachers in Harlem, as an example, can often be heard mouthing words of equality of opportunity to Afro-American and Latino students. These are derived from their own experiences in schools; they tell students that if they work and study hard, they will find rewards and salvation in their adult lives.

Definitions about what is and is not important for youth growing up in the inner city are ignored, and teachers recite a litany of traditional values and beliefs. These seek to define what is good and bad, who is intelligent or stupid, and what good manners ought to be in the classroom. Good taste and the norms of educational decorum are placed in front of children as a constant reproach: this is how you should act if you wish to be considered an intelligent and worthy person. Students are either working at grade level or they are retarded; they either can or cannot master the academic language and culture of the schools. In this manner, the lives that children must live in the meanest conditions are ignored, as are their class struggles to stay alive in a culture that deprives them of their basic necessity—jobs. Children from Harlem are classified and tracked the moment they enter public schools, because such neighborhood schools cater to the poor and outcast of New York. These children do not speak the language or understand the culture of the schools, and the schools are not able to teach them these important skills. Hierarchies are established early, even in these schools that have been structured for failure. Students are locked into tracks from which they seldom escape. The struggle for grades and recognition mimics the social relations of production in adult society, and teachers do little more than reinforce the inevitable failure of minority groups and the poor.

Inner-city schools are suffused with a business ideology: punctuality, hard work, even when the work makes no sense, and an exaggerated respect for authority are valued. Students are judged by their ability to read, write, deport themselves properly, and assimilate the language and culture of the curriculum. The entire enterprise is depicted as an ethical competition, with the prizes going to the most meritorious. To them belong the spoils—access to higher education and better paying jobs in the labor market.

Thus, the teacher-student dynamic has from earliest times concerned itself with discipline, order, control, and an attempt to imitate, as best it could, the boss-worker relationship. The last of these goals is achieved through the autocratic, directive actions of teachers, in which children are taught the appropriate behaviors associated with their subordinate status in the classroom. This is the symbolic order, and it is inevitably accompanied by an ethic or ideology that assures students that the teacher is concerned only with their education and well-being. An example of this can be seen from the following classroom experience, taken from my field notes in an inner-city junior high school:

Teacher: Some of you have asked why I talk about you as disadvantaged students. I'll try to show you why. (Holds up a book end.) Can anyone tell me what this is? (Hands are raised.)

Teacher: Okay, Jerry.

Jerry: It holds your books together on the desk.

Teacher: That's right, Jerry. But what's it called?

Jerry: Called?

Teacher: What's its name?

Jerry: It holds books together. . . . Isn't that enough?

Teacher: No, Jerry. That's not enough. This thing has a name. It's a book end. See what I mean? I knew that when I was five years old!

Most relationships between teachers and students have antagonistic and adversarial features built into them. These are caused by the teacher's need to force students to learn the arbitrary language and culture of the school. Teachers regard the scholastic culture as desirable while rejecting the backgrounds of working-class and racially different children. Racism is seldom mentioned in these classrooms, and the teachers' disinterest in this subject is conveyed by words and deeds. It is of utmost importance that the teacher-boss inculcate the values and beliefs of the social and economic system of the state, since these are the interests she serves; these pay her salary and supervise her work.

Thus, the children of central Harlem's schools are condemned to a career of failure; schooling prepares them for the lesser occupations or the reserve army of labor. Schooling must be described as a process of indoctrination, since it treats such youngsters as ignorant and unworthy failures early in their school careers. Children in lower-middle-class and working-class neighborhood schools have a different but equally stressful experience. Indeed, it is in just such training that teachers prepare themselves to pass on to their future students an unquestioned acceptance of the social order.⁹

The adoption of the primary task of inculcation by schools can be best understood by examining the socially correct attitudes and behaviors of classroom life. Teachers must teach children to accept subordinate positions in the school bureaucracy; they must teach students to accept lower-status positions by relating them to their achievements in the grading system. These are related, in the final instance, to the social relations of production; it is only by studying these that the interests and ideological concerns of state schools can be readily understood. If we remember that schooling is always to be looked at in social and historical contexts, we will resist the Parsonian temptation to see the social world as a regulated mechanism filled with obedient, compliant robots. With these caveats in mind, the structures and practices in public schools must be related to the demands of adult culture. Through the mediation of a state curriculum and language, teachers define what is and is not important; what is and is not worthwhile; what is and is not worth studying and thinking about. Those students who can ingest these ideas and assimilate them succeed in schools; those who cannot fail.¹⁰

The proper attitudes and learnings that emerge in an elementary school in Harlem and one in middle-class suburbia differ considerably. Both are governed by the structure of class relations that affect daily lives in their communities and by the vicious segregation system existing in the United States. A system of symbolic positioning places these two schools (and districts) in opposition, supplying each with ideological justifications for their very different educational experiences and practices. Through their racial and class memberships, the educational and cultural messages of the schools are received differently. For the suburban, middle-class school, the curriculum and practices have a somewhat familiar ring, while for the children and parents of the inner-city school, they are alien and unreal.

And why is this so?

There is some linkage between the marriage and family life of these two communities and the ability of their children to concentrate and succeed in class-biased schools. Economic deprivation has driven many inner-city families apart, and poverty and crime have taken their toll. This affects the way that children live their preschool years and how well they adjust to the competitive ethos of racist, segregated classrooms. Politically, parents in Harlem are weaker than those in our suburban example and less influential in the education of their children. Suburban parents are more likely to be in evidence during the elementary education of their youngsters, although recent community control reforms have changed this pattern.

We should not pretend, however, that the schools reproduce the social and economic classes and ideas of capitalist society without some struggle. The social system is not a well-ordered machine and its actors are not robots, as we mentioned earlier. But the system does have its ideological and cultural messages, and these create a symbolic order that has much to do with the identity and economic destinies of individuals. We could spend much more time on this topic, deriving further points of interest and fresh problems. But we can say that the schools use language as an instrument of symbolic violence and control, tracking children in infancy. They segregate the children of America along racial and class lines; they use an arbitrary curriculum and pedagogy that discriminates against the urban poor, causing them to fail in large numbers; and they prepare children not for their roles in a democratic society but for their experiences in the authoritarian, capitalist workplace. For the moment, we must be satisfied with these characterizations even though they leave aside the assaults on the self-structures of children.

The Constitution of the Individual

Let us now consider the Cartesian subject-object dialectic at the heart of Western philosophy and thought. We know that the human ego was considered the center of the universe in this formulation, creating and recreating itself and the world in which it lived. More recently, structuralists have taken a more critical view of these ideas, rejecting the ego as a subject who acts upon the world. In their view, the subject is transformed from a constituting agent to one who is constituted in the language and culture. He becomes, in the first instances, the consequence of particular practices occurring in families and schools. This is because the creation of individual subjects is performed by symbolic functions and orders that are ideological in their practices and goals. The individual ego no longer validates his existence by referring to his ability to think or acquire knowledge; while he seems to be doing this in his everyday experiences, his unconscious, and the imaginary and symbolic structures of his mind, appear, on reflection, to be the actual "doers," unbeknownst to him. His parents begin these processes by molding his social self to accommodate the world that existed before he was born. While still quite young, he is constituted in the language and unconscious transmissions of family myths and interests. It is easy to see how the child could misperceive these communications as his essential essence or core. Human beings are drawn into this world of symbolism and imagination before they are born and exist in it until they die. They feel their needs intensely and act to satisfy them in everyday life without understanding how such needs were constituted and conveyed to them—especially when they are indoctrinated by ideological state apparatuses having great status and respect in their families and communities. But we cannot forget that these structures seek to fit individuals into slots in the social and economic order, reproducing an existent set of social relations.

Here the familial complexes play themselves out in love and hostility toward parents and siblings. Freud showed us the power of the unconscious as it structured human discourse and experience in these settings; he revealed a human psyche that was fragmented, ambivalent, and in constant conflict with itself. Impulsiveness and drives, rather than reason and self-interests, were in control of human behavior.

Hostile feelings toward loved ones were not the exception but the rule, even though these were often repressed and out of the conscious reach of family members. In the case of the Oedipal complex, which coincided with the child's transition from his natural state to his role as a human child, we cannot fail to notice the powerful influences of language and culture and their ability to create a sense of Otherness. For the young child, everyday experiences are understood as perceptions about the world. He looks at his parents and siblings and behaves in a loving manner toward them, but he does all this as an obvious subject who can act upon the world in which he lives. He sees the world but does not reflect on the differences between what "is" and the images he sees in his head; he reacts to others but does not comprehend the effects of imaginary and symbolic understandings on self-perceptions. The child recognizes himself only when his self-consciousness expands to include others. Even then, his recognition is really an error, a misrecognition of what is actually happening in the process of cognition. In his daily experiences, others appear as individuals who are actors and doers in their own right, subjects who are in command of themselves and their behaviors. But Freud has already shown us that conscious behavior is the exception, not the rule: the unconscious rules in the human psyche. Thus, the child believes in an empty empiricism. He believes that he knows a world he can never know directly and is unaware of the imaginary and symbolic structures ordering and making sense of his life. He accepts ideological explanations that place him at the center of his social reality, causing him to mistake linguistic constructions for essences.

At this point, we can assert again that the role of ideology in family life is essentially conservative and reproductive. Its effects produce people who cannot understand their true relationships to themselves and the relations that exist in their social and economic lives. Cultural arguments and explanations that seem to reveal these relationships are examples of ideologies in action, as they are conveyed by the unconscious structures of speech and language. Such explanations try to make sense of everyday events, giving them a concreteness and rationality that they do not possess. All recognitions of oneself and one's world occur in the imaginary, either through images implanted in the mind or through words structuring human experiences. The real is never more than what is real for the subject, since his perceptions are incomplete images and his relationships constituted in language. But the individual experiences the world directly in his common-sense understanding of things, unaware of the separations that exist between the images and words and the objects and persons themselves.

Thus, if a child recognizes himself, he recognizes an image in a mirror or a string of signifiers that have been used by others to construct his social self. He recognizes the consequences of an ideological production that begins when he is born and is reinforced by state and religious agencies later in his life. The methods used by these ideological state apparatuses are discursive, purporting to portray the real as it exists. Their messages are always couched in the superordination-subordination modality, so that the ideas of parental and state authority are perpetuated. State agencies produce the desired effect when the individual accepts the truth of these ideologies, accepting also the values and beliefs of parents, teachers, and religious leaders. Children become brothers and sisters, students, workers, and parents themselves, thus reproducing the social structure of their people. Through these ideological practices, the social relations of production appear natural and cannot be questioned or replaced. But cultural production does more: its ideological effects have a significant role in constructing the selves of individuals and groups as they struggle to survive in capitalist systems.

At this point, someone will surely dissent. Granting much of what has been said, how can we accept the notion that the self is created in the earliest years of an individual's life? Anyone who has had children can vouch for the correctness of the Oedipal complex in family life. But there are other moments of importance during which time healing and maturation occur. The irrational and fragmentary self is always open to changes.

To children who are learning to find their place in the family, learning a language and culture means attending to word presentations and social structures familiar to them. A child makes little distinction between the two, but these ideological effects have unconscious roots that make it difficult for him to perceive the forces that structure his family and schooling experiences. The parent or teacher who wants to free himself and his children from these cultural productions has a difficult task. How can he produce more enlightened children when he must use the language and culture of his people? How can he urge children to compete in a schooling experience that hides the inequities of a class system?

Let us consider for a moment the class struggle at the center of Marx's theoretical efforts. The struggle between classes, which he described in brilliant detail, spoke of men who were subjects, capable of organizing themselves in a fight against those who dominated them. We must not forget that Marx wanted the working class to become more conscious of itself and of its interests and goals. His workers were subjects in the manner of the cogito: they could think, therefore they could act. They were movers and shakers of the old order, not robots who were governed by the rules and structures of language and culture. Human personality was formed by the dominant social relations of production between those of capital and labor.

Marx never dealt with how individuals were constituted in the social world; he saw reproduction as an economic phenomena, with culture playing a secondary, ideological role. Since his theories focused on class, the individual was not central to his work. However, he did believe that class played a dominant role in the development of the individual's nature and personality. Freud, on the other hand, paid little attention to classes, preferring instead to focus on the individual and his development from nature to civilized person. His findings were considered ahistorical and overly naturalistic: people living in different social systems still experienced the familial complexes uncovered by psychoanalysis. Sexual and aggressive impulses lay at the core of human personality, and class relations were secondary at best. Race and sex were ignored by Marx, who saw the exploited worker as a unisexual individual in the capitalist system. Marxists have since begun to pay more attention to family influences and "human nature," studying their ideological functions and effects. How critical are the first few years of life, and can they be influenced by experiences in later life? Psychoanalysts, in turn, have learned to appreciate language and discourse in their work, understanding how these create ideological tenets that reinforce the class positions of patients. How important is a person's social class, and can the scars of economic exploitation account for many of the deformities found in modern, alienated men and women?

Social scientists trying to fuse these materialist theories into a single doctrine have a difficult job to perform. Some general insights have been gleaned: ideological struggles, a Marxian concept, are intertwined with and inseparable from the material struggles occurring in the families, schools, and workplaces of capitalist societies. Consciousness and ideology merely reflect the power relations that exist there, using the unconscious processes and structures of speech and language to mask the power and force of dominant groups and classes. Ideologies have their own visions of social reality; they see the world as containing the past memories and experiences of families and class positions. Social consciousness is a rarity in Marxism and psychoanalysis; ideology is intertwined with the social structures and practices that have been taught to individuals as mimetic, unconscious givens. It is extremely difficult to change our understanding of power in family relationships, schools, and workplaces because of the symbolic controls and violence built into the pedagogic acts and authority of these apparatuses. Ideology can only be unmasked by linking it to the interests of groups and classes in society, and especially in validating the social relationships people forge at home, in schools, and in the workplace. So the self is formed by the progression of the child from nature to the symbolic order, but it is also affected by this social structure itself. The child's self, then, is formed through language and the interactions he has with parents and siblings. The material world can only be understood in terms of the symbolic functions that humans use to communicate it to one another.

Ideological and cultural effects do tend to mask the economic and social struggles of people, but they cannot be discussed in isolation. Ideologies support the productive sectors in the final analysis, but they also develop out of the autonomous history of families, schools, churches, and so on. Understanding the myths that support capitalist modes of production have not meant an end to ideologies. On the contrary, they have only shown thinkers why such forms of thought were developed in the first instance, and why they are necessary today. The transformation of capitalism will be far more difficult and time consuming than Marx realized, and the psychological nature of man that Freud uncovered makes it reasonable to wonder whether any social system could survive without significant dosages of coercion and exploitation.

5

The Function of Language in Pedagogic Work

Pedagogic work has only one method at its disposal: the Word. Classrooms are a world of words sustained by teachers; they are the site of the cultural class struggle, the place where youngsters are taught the insistent demands of Otherness. For students, the primary Other in the classroom is the teacher. She is the one they must attend to, the one who has the power to decide. She speaks and they listen. She signifies and they attend. When she begins her pedagogic work, she must construct a collective voice of the Other, reflecting the background and levels of attainment of her children. This is necessary if she is to choose words that they can understand. And when she speaks to individuals, she must attend to the Other that they represent for her. It is the internalization of the mores, moral understandings, and language of the classroom that permits students and teachers to speak and to be understood. Yet this is never something that they consciously plan or execute. Quite early in their schooling, children become aware of the Otherness that teachers and students represent; they see these others as individuals who respond to their messages and reflections. But the teacher is the "real Other" in classroom life. Initially, the child transfers attitudes from the attuned mother to the responsible adult in the classroom. Again, the Other in these instances is never an actual person; it is always an unconscious construct in which the Word is located and used by children and teachers alike. The associations between individuals in these situations exist in an imaginary relationship constructed by language. The teacher is identified by signifiers heavily loaded with cultural and political effects. Both she and her students are objectified because they are linguistically constructed; the classroom world would not be possible without cultural and social suppositions that validate traditional practices and status differences. The Other is the agency through which the intersubjective world of schooling and reality in human relationships is made possible. It is a separate, imaginary entity that provides the teacher with a preliminary receiver who can understand and respond to her spoken words. The unconscious, in these instances, is nothing less than the discourse students and teachers have with the Other before they speak to one another. In this sense, the Other plays a deciding role, controlling the thoughts and behavior of all participants.

When a teacher speaks, students are expected to listen. The words she utters set the parameters of the classroom situation and demand some sort of reply, some recognition of her right to speak and decide things. This establishes the relationships between teachers and students and, as far as our experience indicates, never varies. Even the silence of entering students is a reply to the rules and regulations of Otherness in classroom life and extends to student behavior throughout the day. The teacher listens, hearing what the silence conveys. She smiles at this evidence of her unrestricted authority. When she does speak, her words have a specific function: they teach her students the language and culture of subordination, contrasting their language and culture to that of the educated classes. We underestimate these learnings at our peril, since they teach children to accept submission and the social relations of classroom life and the labor market. They prepare students to be good, obedient, deferential workers after they finish their schooling.

Yet this authority and right to decide sits uneasily upon the teacher's head, forcing her to attend to any slight or misbehavior. She may wonder, at times, what her charges would really say about her if they could speak their minds. At other times, she may project her own forgotten memories and emotions into her thoughts, transferring them from her own childhood experiences. In any case, she will find herself forced to speak and listen constantly. Her words will become repetitive, even to her; they will speak of her need to dominate and control every movement and behavior in her classroom.

What, then, do students want to convey with their servile silence and submissive gestures? They seek to soften the coerciveness and authority of the all-powerful adult, summoning up and transferring behaviors and identifications from previous experiences with all-powerful parents. But mostly, the student seeks recognition and acceptance as a worthwhile and competent person; he seeks some measure of assurance and predictability in his relationship with the demanding teacher.

"A very good answer!" a schoolteacher says, assuming the familiar role of the all-knowing authority. She might think she is giving her students encouragement and praise but is unaware of the dangers such words create, dangers of dependency and submissiveness. She knows nothing of ego-specific forms of praise and is concerned only with order and control, with a quiet and busy classroom. Later, this teacher may relax a bit, once her students have shown that they have no intention of challenging her decisional rights in the classroom.

It is not so surprising that the schoolteacher should show these overriding concerns with order and control and the deportment of her students. From the moment she begins her student teaching, she finds herself in an apprentice situation; she learns to teach the way others have taught before her, the way she was taught when she was a child. She learns to see the children and classroom through the eyes of old-timers who also learned their trade as teaching apprentices. If she challenges the mores and moral understandings of teachers, if she disputes their words, she will be seen as a deviant or worse, and her chances of completing a successful training will be reduced. If, on the other hand, she follows blindly, her first experiences will be more positive, even as she prepares to sustain the arbitrary practices and curriculum of an educational system in perpetual crises.

Later she may come to understand the nature of her educational discourses with teachers and professors of education; she may glimpse the force that supports her pedagogic actions and authority in state schools. Her methods will be shaped by the words of others who have come before her and seek to reproduce the social relations of educational production. For the teacher's pedagogic actions are, first and foremost, a form of pedagogic control and violence.[1] They need to be learned over and over again by new teachers who want to "help" children and who do not understand that state schools are dedicated to inculcation and little else. The teacher is an agent of the state and a conveyor of the social mores and power systems of the school and workplace. As such, she must teach an arbitrary curriculum and use age-old pedagogic practices if she is to fulfill the educational system's tasks of educational and social reproduction.[2]

How, then, are we to understand the actual conditions of pedagogic practice in state schools? Are all efforts by teachers forms of symbolic control and violence? Or do they have other, more beneficent effects? The ideas that are most often associated with pedagogic actions in state schools are "rote" learning and an exaggerated respect for authority figures. These have been the catch phrases of educators for centuries, attesting to their awareness of the hidden hostility and adverse reactions of students to their constant, impositional behaviors. By routinizing classroom life, the teacher trains her students to sit in their seats, to place their coats on numbered hooks, and so on. She teaches them to enter the room in an orderly and quiet manner, talking to no one. Children are not to chew, fight, or throw things. They are not to leave their desks or talk without permission. And they must always be willing and able to give an account to teachers of their presence in any part of the school building.

The fact remains, however, that these practices have unintended effects. When we observe classroom behaviors, we can often sense the frustration welling up in teachers and students as they try to sustain these unnatural and repressive relationships. We can see students squirm as they suppress their need for social intercourse, occasionally breaking rules and causing aggressive responses from teachers. Students will sometimes react angrily to the arbitrary behavior of instructors, calling out at inappropriate times during the lesson or hassling others near them. But most often, they regress into docility and silent hostility while teachers transfer behaviors from their own schooling experiences to their students. This is to be expected when children are deprived of social and educational needs in mass schools and ordered about as though they were inmates in maximum-security prisons. The gulf between teachers and students has always been a wide one, and it continues to widen still.

Schooling seems unable to deal with these weaknesses in its pedagogic practices, primarily because they serve social functions not consciously perceived by teachers and students. Both tend to make sense of their situations, accepting ideological definitions of themselves and the work they do together. But the teacher has particular problems that frustrate her best efforts to help her students. What are the sources of her frustration? For one thing, she can never know what lies behind the obedient silence and deference her students afford her. An answer or response will often convey a disapproving or disinterested gesture, or silence will hinder her efforts to make a disciplinary or pedagogical point. Again, the curriculum at the center of the learning situation is alien and has been developed by others who are far away from her classroom and its children. The rote remembrance of facts leads to a boring educational discourse. The "facts" help students to do better on tests, but they have little or no relevance to their lives and cause them to disengage further from their own education.

Students are engaged in a learning experience that seems incoherent and contradictory at best. Pedagogic actions teach them to see themselves as incompetent persons who are unable to control themselves or learn the things that they need to know. Their narcissistic selves come into conflict with the institutional identity assigned to them on the basis of their ability to read and understand the Word as it is conveyed by educational authorities. Now the student begins to see himself in racial, sexual, and intellectual roles that were less relevant in his preschool environments. His feelings about himself and his kinfolk are undermined, as is his confidence in himself. In the classroom, he must maintain his student identity, alienating and making himself over to fit the definitions of others. The ego of the student is meant to bear these frustrations, assuring that its line of action is the most reasonable one under the circumstances. But this leads to inevitable feelings of anger and frustration, since it forces the student to give up his needs and desires. The student makes himself an object for his teacher and the educational system by adopting the demeanor and behavior of the submissive role in the school environment. He cannot find satisfaction in these poses, since they demean him (and his family). This is why he tends to withdraw during classroom lessons, seeking to preserve as much of his personal self as he can. He may be unaware of how his identity is constituted by language, but he becomes aware, over time, of the variance between his personal and student selves.

The aggressive behaviors accompanying coercive classroom practices are not focused on social and personal needs alone. Student aggressiveness deals with deeper responses associated with relationships between parent and child and boss and worker. It is a response to the teacher's overt disapproval and disrespect for the youngster's efforts. However, open student resistances are not tolerated in classrooms and transpose themselves into fantasies and passivity in the face of insistent questions and demands.

Let us return now to the teacher and her pedagogic work. She has her suppositions when she enters the classroom; she has her imaginary intentions, and these are attached to symbolic understandings of the pedagogic act. "I am here to serve my students," she tells herself. "I am here to teach them." These are the assumptions of her own role and identity and the source of much of her frustration in the classroom. The teacher cannot understand her true relationship to students as long as she ignores her role as a state worker, as long as she is ignorant of the social functions of schooling in modern life. The problems become acute when a teacher begins to comprehend how ineffective she often is and develops negative feelings, first toward herself, and then, adopting the paranoid slant, toward the children who seem to thwart her best efforts. She begins her work with an acute awareness of her ineffectiveness and ignorance and ends by blaming her failures on the students themselves. But this is a process that takes some time, during which her certitudes about herself and her work undergo radical transformations. And it is through the constant discourses with her peers and students that she arrives at these ideas, crystallizing and maintaining the separation that exists between her and the children she is supposed to serve.

As long as the teacher takes her pedagogic work at face value, she is condemned to frustration and confusion. Her words are greeted with growing silence and passivity by students; their gestures and behavior are controlled by a need to mask frustrations and anger until they are out of the sight and hearing of school authorities. Of course, the classroom is nothing if it is not constant communication. The teacher decides what is to be discussed and studied while the students can only react to these decisions. Even if the lessons are boring and irrelevant, they affirm the teacher's authority to speak and decide in the classroom. To get some sense of these practices, we must turn our attention to those elements of the pedagogic act that are most familiar to us. And the easiest way to access this material will be to examine actual classroom encounters which I have recorded in my notebooks over the past thirty years.

This morning I made my first visit to one of the reading teachers in our middle school. At the front of her class sat Mrs. Harris, the principal's favorite teacher! Her face was very tense, and her eyes bulbous behind thick spectacles. She seemed anxious and displeased to see me. Every student sat upright in their seats. (She must be doing something right, I told myself.) A boy walked up and down the aisles giving out materials. To one side, a second monitor checked attendance while students prepared for work. A very well-disciplined class! Very attentive!

Finally, Mrs. Harris spoke. In a flat, metallic voice, she said: "Turn to page 74 and read pages 74 through to page 83. Then complete the questions on page 83 in your notebooks. Any questions? Begin!"

At her word, books were opened, and eyes began to read. I was surprised that no attempt was made to motivate the reading or review difficult vocabulary words. The children hadn't been asked to speculate about the title of the story or what they might be reading about. Still, everyone seemed to be working! Mrs. Harris was working, too. She sat in the front of the room doing clerical chores! I didn't know what to do. After a few moments, I began to move about the room. Several students didn't have any idea about what they were reading. Others didn't know key words and concepts. They scribbled and drew pictures in their notebooks or just stared out the window. After almost 30 minutes, everyone was asked to turn back to page 74. Then each student read a paragraph while the other children followed along by pointing to each word as it was read aloud. At that point, I left the room. If this was the way our more experienced teachers were teaching, what could we expect from our new recruits?

The element in this pedagogic encounter that stood out most was the teacher's decisional rights in the classroom: she announced what the activity would be and when it would begin and end. This arose from her position as the legal-rational authority in the classroom situation. She was the representative of the state, and, as such, she had the authority and power over her students. The "reading" lesson immediately revealed its connection to the rituals and traditions of public schooling itself. From the moment they came into the classroom, the students were engaged in waiting behavior, even though they were not permitted to speak or leave their seats. The figure of the teacher further reminded them that she was the important person; she was the one who would initiate the learning situation. This lesson was actually a text on how not to teach—the teacher failed to perform many acts of good pedagogy. She did not move about to see if her students needed help; she did not individualize her instruction in any way, giving everyone the same assignment. And these were only the most obvious failures. Of greater significance were the implications of these actions for her students. Many felt confused and deeply troubled by their experiences in her classroom. They were only "going through the motions" during this period and didn't learn much. The teacher's words were also revealing; she permitted questions but did not try to encourage students to actually speak. Once she had told them what to do, further communication was not needed. This reaffirmed the relevant membership categories of the participants. The teacher sat at a desk on a podium, high above the students. She used a surveillance method of control, looking up from time to time to see if students were absorbed in their schoolwork. She could see who was looking at the pages in the book and who was not following her instructions.

It is easy to see how aggressive and unpleasant feelings develop between teachers and students, as they pursue their imaginary intentions in the classroom. This is the core of the resistance teachers face when they perform their pedagogic duties, reducing students to submissive and passive automatons. The teacher is burdened with anxiety as she tries to maintain order and control in such environments, as she forcibly intervenes in classroom life. Whether or not her efforts will end in some beneficial happenings for students in the future is beside the point. Their present experience is characterized by pedagogic encounters insufficiently explained and irrelevant to their lives outside of school.

The imaginary intentions of the teacher are expressed in symbolic terms (and ideologies): she is there to educate, to help children learn what they must know to succeed in adult life. Few teachers know about inculcation and the true nature of their work in state schools. "I have acted like this in the interests of my students," one teacher in the South Bronx told me, justifying her impositional behaviors. Such righteous attitudes and anxieties stem from normative beliefs and duties. The teacher must impose the state curriculum on disinterested children in a competitive ethos.

The danger for the teacher is always the same; it is that the negative reactions of the students will lead to chaos and anarchy, or worse. She must repress awareness of her less helpful behaviors: yelling at children, scolding them, humiliating them, disgracing them in front of others, evaluating their work, and grading them in ways that cause them to drop out or fail. The certitudes of the teacher are steeped in folklore and tradition and supported by an apprenticelike tenure that perpetuates archaic practices. And it is in these ideological issues that insights must be sought. Significantly, teachers always respond to criticisms with anger, denying the effects of their behavior on the selves of children. This is because they wish to take the schooling of children at face value, without looking into the actual and unintended effects of education in racist, class-biased, and sexist schools. They perform their work with myriads of others who accept without thought the mores and moral understandings of state schools. Again, the Word is used to mask the role of the state, giving schooling an aura of altruism and autonomy that it does not possess.

Even if teachers are unaware of their role in the inculcation process, words are their only way of performing their pedagogic functions. As they deny the obvious, they affirm the words they have grown up with as students, student teachers, and teachers. The results of their practices may point to failure and deception, but they continue to support traditional ways of dealing with children in overcrowded, mass schools. This is the system their parents believed in, and they accept it, too. Moreover, our analysis must focus on the speech that conveys the ethical justifications for imitative, impositional behaviors in classrooms. Here we must introduce the bizarre orientation sequences teachers experienced in an inner-city junior high school.[3]

Today we met the new bunch of teachers, and they were mostly college kids with no experience in ghetto schools! Just out of school themselves! Mostly they sat around long tables and waited. A few read the materials we had given them and talked to one another. Others just sat by themselves and smoked. An assistant principal passed out more materials, and then we waited some more. Everyone leaned forward when the principal entered and began his welcoming speech. The next week these young people would be in the middle of a ghetto school.

"At first," he was saying, "you'll be confused. You won't know what to do. You'll make mistakes. Don't worry. Everyone does, at first. . . . You'll flounder. After all, what do you know about teaching? You've been in the learner's seat all your life!" Several of the young teachers moved uncomfortably in their chairs. "What should you do?" (Hands were raised in the audience.) "No, no! Don't raise your hands. This isn't kindergarten! Don't talk! Just listen! I'll tell you what to do. . . ."

"Pick out someone on our staff who seems to know what he's doing. A veteran. . . . Then, do what he does. Walk like him. Talk like him. And soon, you'll be like him! Watch the way he gets out of his car in the morning, and then, you do it the same way. Study how he reacts under stress, and then, you do it the same way. Study the way he controls his classes, and then, you do it the same way. And before you know it, the words and actions will become your words and actions, and you'll be an effective teacher, too!"

The speech caused quite a stir. Teachers coughed nervously and cast their eyes downward. Was he serious? Or was this a joke of some kind? Imitate the behavior of veteran teachers, and you would make it in a ghetto school? Could that work? Could college students just out of the university plan meaningful experiences for ghetto youth by imitating the behavior and speech of others? Could they win the respect and affection of their students that way?

The principal insisted upon addressing new teachers by their surnames. By doing so, he hoped to alert them to what they probably knew: in the school, they would be the responsible persons. They would have to give up personal feelings and identities to assume the role and demeanor of the teacher. This would require that they define every situation inside the building. And their ability to do so would be central to their maintenance of order and control. Children would be told who they were, where they were, why they were there, and what they were supposed to do while they were there. When the students accepted the teacher's right to decide, then it would be possible to construct the elements of a learning situation. The only acceptable responses from students were deference and obedience.

The principal seemed frustrated by these new teachers, and he let them know it. He moved about quite a bit and turned his eyes upward in disgust when they tried to answer his questions. His voice oozed condescension: he would have to start from the beginning with these raw recruits. His manner also indicated that he would not tolerate any idealistic notions about what the teaching situation would be like. He was like a sergeant talking to recruits before they were sent into action, and his pauses suggested that he was choosing his words carefully! That these newcomers would come to see things through the eyes of old-timers was only a matter of time, he told them. They were "snot-noses" now, but those who did not drop out would learn how to survive in the ghetto school; they would learn that they were the responsible ones in a stressful situation.

The Language of Devaluation

Turning now to students, we can see that regression is easily observable in classrooms; it is the decomposition of a student's fantasy relations with the commanding adult. The regression is not real in the clinical sense. Once the student is free of the classroom, he easily reverts to his personal identity. Still, he regresses to earlier dependent behaviors so that he can navigate through the demands of the pedagogic experience. As an infant and child, the youngster learns many social and linguistic skills during his preschool years, but in schools, he is asked to regress to the passive, silent state of infancy. He is asked to obey without thought, preparing him for his later role as the good worker in capitalist society.

It is for this reason that teachers mislead themselves when they direct attention to the reality of the pedagogic moment. The rules of classroom life exclude open intercourse between teachers and students, forcing both to play-act their roles. Again, the student-teacher apprenticeship sharpens the dichotomy between these two groups and assures their common alienation from one another. Even the supervisory controls of teachers makes it less likely that they will learn anything substantial about their students' needs and desires. Under their guidance, the students appear to know less and less as they progress through the school system, showing little willingness to read a book on their own or study at home. "School's out!" they will tell their parents when asked why they never study or read. Thus, the legal and educational efforts of society end in apparent failure; students read less and less as they grow older and do less well in school. They are forced to resist the impositions and definitions of teachers, defending themselves in any way that they can. Teachers control students in classrooms, divining their authority from state licenses and societal traditions. But they cannot educate children, they cannot teach them to love learning in such coercive, alienating environments.

The nature of the teacher's work is therefore always focused on the curriculum and away from the individual needs of the students they "serve." Not only are the words and behavior of youngsters determined by the decisions of the teacher but their actions are constantly evaluated and recorded for further assessment and placement. Tracking leads those students who fail into a stigmatized and unrewarding educational experience. Millions drop out at an early age, happy to be out of school. Some teachers do try to concern themselves with the imaginary relationships that develop between them and their students, but these efforts are not supported by educational authorities. In most instances, they learn the language and moral understandings of the teaching profession, paying closer attention to social control and standardized test scores. They fail to grasp how students transfer feelings from past situations to their teachers, and how teaches develop countertransferences that also confound the relationships that develop in classrooms. Without such insights, teaches can never understand what is happening to them and their students; they can never understand what is behind the behavior of youngsters.

Students use the Word to respond to pedagogic commands. They seek to avoid constant corrections and humiliations in front of peers, splitting their identities and becoming students who stifle their inner needs and desires. They seem vaguely aware that the pedagogical act is suffused with subjugation and a devaluation of themselves and their personal heritages. After all, they are in training to take the places of workers who will soon be too old to work.

If we remember our history of education in the United States, we have to admit that the schools have organized themselves around arbitrary pedagogic practices and an obsessive concern with student submissiveness and obedience. Progress for students has involved meaningless work; the child's nature must be made to accept, without question, this boring work and the social relations of educational production as they exist in state schools. The arbitrary and authoritarian practices of schooling have been in sharp contrast to its ideological pretensions. Its language has divided and separated the classes, defining students according to their race, sex, and ethnicity and making a mockery of equal access and opportunity. Nothing has taught students the ethos of submission more effectively than having to mind the words of their "betters" for such a long training period. It has been in the speech and language of the child that the teacher has found the means and the will to classify him, discerning who he is and who his parents are in the larger social world. Using a tone of command, chastising students in front of others, separating them according to their deportment and academic attainments—each of these archaic practices has a part in preparing youth for the authoritarian workplaces awaiting them in the adult world.

Resistances and Failures

When we look at it from these perspectives, it becomes clear why schooling is such a traumatic experience. If these pedagogic practices are the cause of student resistances and failures, it is because they put into words the difficulties children experience when they face the colossus—the educational bureaucracy. And these words are written down in cumulative files that become the child in the eyes of the administration, affecting students throughout their school careers. Verbalization has its own reality, and it interacts with social constructions to present teachers and students with a set of givens and suppositions that they cannot ignore. Through language, the past is remembered and passed on. Teachers react to the words of students, classifying them and separating the good from the bad. They simply attend to their vocabularies and syntax, despising those who are "disadvantaged" and unable to master the academic curriculum. Children find themselves constructed in the language of teachers, coming to see themselves as "bad actors," "remedial cases," or worse. And this is carried out constantly in classroom discourses, which permit students' failures to be known to parents and peers, and later to other teachers. Thus, his cumulative record, containing evidence of previous indiscretions and failures, alerts new teachers to the problems a student may present for them.

Pedagogic action is, above all, a spoken representation of the social relations of schools and society often with discouraging and unpleasant results. Through it, students are subjected to ideological communications that mask the nature of their relations in schools and classrooms. Words fix youngsters in their place, preparing them for a destiny that they are often unable to influence. They are seen as born into meager circumstances, or disadvantaged, because of their ethnic and racial heritage. Perhaps a more supportive environment could cause these outcasts to achieve more in their school careers. But the competitive, impersonal ethos of state schools causes them to get lost in the shuffle, failing in incredible numbers and dropping out at early ages.

These words, which recall the failures of children, move between the imaginary and the real, confounding the behavior of teachers and students alike. Teachers think they know a child once they have read his cumulative file or after they have seen him in "action" for a day or two. But the real in these instances is only what is real for these teachers and often omits acts of courage and bravery children reveal as they attend impersonal and penal-like schools with surprising dignity and grace. Even the hostility of pedagogic practices are ignored by the teacher, since she sees her impositional actions as helpful. Not that the perceptions of the teacher are completely in error. But the language she uses tends to separate her from those students who need guidance and understanding most. For the Word that structures classroom discourses testifies to the past, in an incomplete and biased way. It is accepted as reality only because the Word bears witness to past transgressions, giving them a concreteness that they never possessed. Teachers take for granted the restructuring of past events in words, without realizing that the words are not the experiences themselves and that teacher provocations and countertransferences are often omitted from these transcriptions. What is more, the time intervals and maturation of students are ignored in these educational practices, and youngsters are often forced to begin new classroom experiences with teachers who have been unduly influenced by past records.

Thus, pedagogic actions use the Word and structures created by the Word in the past, conferring meaning and intentions on practices that are grounded in ideologies and traditions. Its methods are continuous discourses, during which time the world is made into an intelligible and understandable whole. This is accomplished by forcing a transindividual, imaginary reality on students, who must either master and internalize it or fail in their academic work. Pedagogic actions use social histories and memories to structure classes and stratify students. When the child enters the state school for the first time, he commits himself to an institutional identity and training: he agrees to play the student role at all times during his life inside the school building. This agreement is supported by state law, which commands him to attend no matter what his experiences or failures. Now he becomes the ignorant one who needs instruction; now he becomes the unformed mind who requires adult guidance and molding; now he is the undisciplined one who must be watched at all times; now he is the childish one who needs to be taught how to work, how to do what he is told without resistances or questions. And this student identity is constituted in an intersubjective world in which youngsters must be deferential and submissive to adult mentors who "know what is good for them."

The Role of the Unconscious

It will be seen on reflection that the unconscious, through speech and language, plays a commanding role in the social structures and practices of educational systems. The unconscious is the means through which transindividual communications are made possible in classrooms and schools; it is the universal signification system that teachers and students share when they begin work together. The unconscious is above and beyond the reality of individuals, providing them with ideas and thoughts that make the schooling situation possible. These are freed from formal logic and rationality, even as they often pay lip service to consciousness.

The unconscious is that part of an educational system's history that is marked by mythology, folklore, and amnesia. It is the proscribed past that has forgotten its own roots and social functions. The unconscious can be seen in the huge public buildings that house our educational efforts—impersonal edifices without character that reveal the structure of schooling like inscriptions on ancient relics and ruins. The unconscious reveals itself also in the cumulative files and bureaucratic documents wherein impenetrable memories of the past exist, away from the conscious knowledge of present-day teachers and students.

The unconscious can be uncovered in the words and phrases that teachers and students use when they speak to one another. The observances that occur in school buildings are rooted in understandings that have been passed on from generation to generation, and that still have vitality in spite of great changes in student backgrounds and economic progress. The unconscious can be discerned in the traditions and folklore of schooling, and in the normative and ethical structures used to validate pedagogic practices. It also exists in the ideologies that, in traditional forms, transform the history of state schools and mask their failure to educate silent armies of immigrant and poor children.

Finally, the unconscious makes itself known in the contradictions existing between the goals and outcomes of public schools. It can be found in the distortions made necessary by the history of education in modern times, and in the discrepancies between its ideological aspirations and the requirements of modern capitalist systems. The history of ideas leads to a historization of schooling, which occurred before such thoughts were written down. These carry unintended and unknown messages from forgotten social experiences in the past. This history of education is still another instance of schooling's unconscious: every historical trauma and success represent a forgotten page of glory or failure that resonates in the social and educational practices of schools. What has been forgotten about schooling's roots is remembered in its language and actions, and these suggest penal and military institutions and a regimenting mentality. The unconscious of educational systems is the Otherness that greets teachers and students when they enter schools and begin to interact with one another, unaware of the power that people far away from their classroom wield over them.

Schooling becomes a given to teachers and students; the buildings and cumulative records cannot be ignored. These affect the motivation and achievement of students and the efforts of teachers. A youngster may begin his schooling after a preschooling period during which reading and writing skills were not emphasized; he may never have seen a book before, and his teeth may ache because he has never seen a dentist. He may find himself hungry in the morning and during his first hours in school, and his parents may not speak English as their primary language. Or they may speak in a way that absolutely classifies them, in the words of George Bernard Shaw, identifying their lower-class position in society. Because these events and understandings are revealed in language, the student may never see how they affect his chances, and the teacher may only understand these variables in a superficial way.

The unconscious, in these circumstances, is a symbolic order, defining individuals without their awareness, without their understanding of the effects it has on discourses and destinies. Often, it appears as traditional practices, reflecting the social mechanisms developed to deal with problems that occurred in the distant past. These mechanisms have remained intact and seem to have an impetus or life of their own. What schools teach children is the history of social and economic structures they might have experienced if they had lived more than thirty years ago. But this history is presented as a guide to the present; it is presented as facts, not as words that have censored and interpreted past events.

Every experience of failure and rejection in classrooms leaves personal scars. The humiliation of these early student experiences are often repressed and unavailable for conscious retrieval; the successes, when they come, are inflated. But what has been forgotten still exists and affects the way students and teachers act in present-day classrooms.

When students progress through the grade system, the structures of schooling seem to have a permanence and logic to them that cannot be denied. The Word has the function of structuring these social realities into eternal verities. The problems associated with age-segregation practices are seldom discussed, and children move through the system regardless of individual needs or preferences. When they need older students to help them through difficult stages in their development, they are often not available. The competitive, class-bound ethos of schooling presents children with a predetermined destiny that is very difficult to overcome.

Teachers are a major factor in these educational practices, in spite of constant denials. Their training, as we have mentioned, makes it difficult for them to teach children from different cultural and linguistic backgrounds. The profession's practices are steeped in tradition and folklore, not in scientific theory or research. They do teachers little honor and are reflected in the low status and pay teachers receive for their efforts. Passing on the values and beliefs of the state, these practices transform schools into inculcation systems that transmit and validate the power and culture of the business classes.

Normative Order and Empirical Conflict in Schools and Society

What are the normative features supporting these arbitrary and impositional educational practices? How do they support the modern capitalist state? To answer such questions, we must begin with an analysis of civil society's need for tolerable levels of equilibrium and control in the streets, workplaces, and schools. We must recognize the teacher's overriding concern for order and her need to be constantly reassured that she has, in fact, the right to wield power and authority in her classroom. It will be seen, on closer consideration, that order is necessary if the everyday life of classrooms and civil society are to maintain a tolerable balance, if conflicts are to be held to a minimum.[4] Teachers and business and political leaders face certain political and economic challenges to the order they impose upon others. Their responses differ according to the nature and intent of the challenges they face. An analysis of such responses must transcend instrumental conceptualizations of class, language, and rationality. Both civil society and schools hold certain assumptions, certain normative suppositions and expectations that are carried over from other civilizations. It is through a dynamic interaction between these linguistic and cultural expectations and normative assumptions that an empirical order is allowed to emerge in classrooms and society. The conflict that develops out of the struggle of individuals and classes to change their present-day economic and social conditions occurs within the context of symbols and ideologies that have been internalized and passed on from one generation to the next.

It is essential to understand the environment within which these conflicts occur before we can grasp their multidimensional nature and our tendency to misinterpret them. The classroom is more than a mere representation or replication of the densely populated urban centers in which economic and social life occurs. In Max Weber's words, cities include political-territorial aspects as well as economic-market ones. The classroom is the smaller sphere, where these conditions are reproduced along with political-territorial features, although these are most often obscured by the blustering authority of teachers. Everything in classrooms has its corollary in the workplace; although economic-market features in classroom life are subtle and difficult to ascertain, they become more apparent when pedagogic actions are related to sociocultural functions in modern society. Until we look at the language and culture that is perpetuated by the schools and contrast it with the language and culture of students, we cannot understand the class and knowledge stratification functions that schools perform in mass culture.

The school must therefore be understood to include the political, economic, and social aspects of civil society. This is important if we are to set aside its ideological effects. The autonomy of educational systems is never more than an apparition, since their primary purpose in society is to reproduce the social relations that exist in schools and the workplace. Citizens accept schooling because they believe in the egalitarian ideologies that support such institutions. They believe that schooling will improve the possibilities for their children, even as statistics indicate otherwise. For educational systems in capitalist society, this ideological effect is important, since the pervasiveness of state bureaucracies allows them to appear as autonomous agencies without parallel in other societies. This appearance of independence is vital to the ideology of schooling as an impartial and fair adjudicator of student progress and development, allowing individuals from different classes in society to accept the notion of equal access and preparation for all citizens. But subjective and communal ties have always bound individuals to their class, their ethnic group, and their political allegiances.

To understand these ties, Weber has challenged us to analyze the normative features supporting the social and educational systems of a particular social formation. For capitalism, the focus is on understanding the consequences of material change and the uneven distribution of wealth; the religious explanations that inhibit or aid in the development of secular science; and the use of prophecy and nonrational thought in the everyday living experiences of citizens. The cities and schools of previous civilizations created universalistic associations in some instances and failed to do so in others. Weber writes that these associations were fraternal in essence and often familial as well. Men and women were either from the city or from the country; the concept of citizen came later and tended to differentiate individuals from both of these types. In modern capitalist society, the concept of the urban worker and entrepreneur had a long history in European development and played a commanding role in the development of schooling.

The development of the burgher citizen had profound consequences for the economic structures and distribution systems that preceded the establishment of state schools in advanced capitalist countries. The results were complicated by the development of the urban proletariat, or worker, concept that tended to bring people together from different social, economic, and cultural backgrounds. These newcomers were members of no kin groups save those of their previous native villages. Their cultural remembrances were filled with religious and cult associations and rigid class affiliations. Attempts to organize these urban workers into unions ran into the barriers of their previous understandings and normative values, which opposed universalistic associations. Economic classes were formed in capitalist cities and states, composed of burghers who were all deemed to be citizens of equal weight before the law. These citizens were seen as individuals, an abstract legal definition that had no basis in the previous life experiences of rural folk who had migrated to the towns and cities. The tribe or clan or familial relations of the past were now superseded by a less satisfying, less enveloping legal status of citizen. In the state schools, this identity was transformed into students, all of whom were seen to be equal in the eyes of the law, all of whom were given equal opportunities to succeed.

According to Weber, the differences that developed between these citizens were to be traced not to their economic conditions but to their comparative religious understandings and cultural backgrounds. Christianity, as the supreme example, was able to develop a religious community that transcended the relationships of family and class. And this was reflected in the schools, where everyone was able to attain the status of student and Christian citizen, regardless of previous statuses in their countries of origin. Barriers of birth and community were abolished, and all immigrants to the United States, as one example, were given the title of American—that is, citizen. Thus, the power of kinship groups and clans was significantly weakened, and the beliefs of the individual became his primary entree into religious and civil society.

Weber believed that the development of the Western city and state involved revolution, during which time the lower classes or strata were spurred into action by normative ideals that were associated specifically with the burgher ascendancy. This began to occur during the twelfth century, when urban merchants started to have serious conflicts with the aristocratic classes and culture. The new burgher classes used their citizenship under the normative order to define their rights and privileges in the city and state. The normative changes in perception were accompanied by changes in the material conditions of the burgher class, which further encouraged them to participate in the development of civic power that was to become decisive during the next centuries. As with the aristocratic classes, the burghers were separated from the poor of society by their ability and willingness to pay taxes. But their conflict with the nobility developed over their rights as commoners and citizens. A normative egalitarianism developed in these new cities that now spoke of the rights and changes that were needed if trade and commerce were to flow freely. Once the confidence of the burghers reached a certain point, they could no longer tolerate being seen as beneath the lazy, oafish types that predominated in much of the nobility.

The educational systems began to reflect the changes in the economic and social distribution structures of the new burgher culture. The urban proletariat was won over by ideological promises of freedom, equality, and fraternity, bringing people of the national state together and schooling them in common schools. While it is true that the class divisions in society were still reflected in the education and language of individuals and their families, these were masked by economic associations that seemed less oppressive than those of the feudal period. Attempts to train children in state schools provided nation-states with normative and emotional ties that created patriotic emotions and beliefs. This training produced substitute workers and citizens willing and able to take their places in the economic system as it was. All children were eventually enrolled in these state schools, and they were supposedly evaluated by their academic attainments rather than by their birth into particular families and classes.

The economic, cultural, and religious ties of individuals provided them with starting points in their educational careers; those with economic, cultural, and linguistic advantages soon pulled ahead in the competitive ethos of burgher schools. Nevertheless, all were treated as equals, even though the stratification practices weeded out the children of the poorer classes in the elementary grades.

Schools became an important institution in burgher society, taking over many of the inculcation functions performed by the family and church in precapitalist periods. The rights and privileges of a business society were emphasized by constant discourse in classrooms, along with an affirmation of its ideological and cultural perspectives.

6

The Imaginary World of the Classroom

The imaginary is inseparable from the symbolic. It allows the child to see himself as the center of a knowable universe; without him, nothing has meaning or importance, nothing exists. He sees the world "out there," surrounding him with images, and does not understand that "out there" is really inside his brain. He is completely egocentric and unable to see himself as one of many in any situation. Images and ideas lie dormant until he focuses on them; then they must be translated into words before they can be retrieved. Perceptions themselves are deeply influenced by the language and culture of his family. These define everything and everyone, causing him to see things through the eyes of his parents and providing him with suppositions that prepare him for future events in his life.

A child will often be told about school before he ever attends one, before he ever sets foot in a classroom. From this, he imagines that he knows what goes on there, what will happen when schooling begins. The imaginary function of the mind permits him to engage in an intersubjective world of language, even though he has never had such an experience before. It allows him to be perceived as an other by fellow students and his teacher. For them, he is a boy, a student, a friend, and so on. This happens as soon as he and an Other engage in pleasure-seeking or competitive discourses. The imaginary makes it possible for the individual to perceive and relate segments of the real world to one another. In this way, it creates a misrecognition of the real, causing the individual to believe that there are connections and relationships where none may exist, or where they are quite beyond his understanding.

It would scarcely do if we were to ignore the relationships between the imaginary and symbolic orders: both are genetic and structural concepts that Jacques Lacan used in diverse and ambiguous ways. They mark the transition from the natural state after childbirth to the human one at about age three. From the mirror experiments, we have learned how the infant comes to recognize himself and others; from the Oedipus complex, we have become more sensitive to the child's entrance into the symbolic world of his parents. In the mirror experiments, the infant's primary relationships were with the nurturing Other. But in these early months, he seems unable to differentiate himself from this Other or from any others he sees in the glass. Later, he is able to make these distinctions; familial tensions and conflicts force him into self and other identifications, disturbing his imaginary fantasies and making him fit into the symbolic order of language and civilization. Now he becomes an object for others. Now he can identify himself and others, aware that his sex, race, and place in his family are important features of his personal identity. Things have names and so do people; he learns to see himself as a child in the demanding world of sibling rivals and adults.

The mastery of language and the infant's entrance into the life of the family are two critical moments in his development. They take him from the imaginary to symbolic situations that are influenced by the imaginary. He is forced to attend to familial experiences and those of his immediate neighborhood. Without him, as we have said, such phenomena have little or no significance or meaning, even though he may acknowledge their existence upon reflection. He experiences the world directly, mystically, giving it meaning and remaining unconcerned with philosophical questions and epistemology. These common-sense understandings are controverted by the work of scholars, as we have seen. They have taught us that human beings perceive and interpret the world through unconscious processes, forcing order and rationality on an essentially disorderly and chaotic universe. Freud has shown that the individual does not have control over his own behavior, and that human consciousness is a rarity.[1]

Imaginary functions play an important part in the meanings people attach to their lives and the world in which they live. Individuals need reasons for the lives they lead each day; they employ imaginary capabilities to explain away such fundamental anxieties as chronic illnesses and death. Reality is too complex and devious for them to fathom; no one person can ever grasp its nuances and true conditions. The imaginary leads to the ideological because the individual needs to understand the conditions of his life. He needs to make them tolerable at the very least. In the symbolic order, the contradictory, immense universe is explained, along with the person's place in it. Man sees himself as the subject at the center of the social and physical reality and discourses from which his thoughts and behavior have originated. Expressing itself through the medium of language, the imaginary presents the real world as a unified whole and ignores or denies inconsistencies and contradictions. Both the person and the world are seen as a totality, a universe allowing for immediate and accurate perception and cognition by knowing individuals.

But people also perceive and interpret the world through the prism of imaginary cultural backgrounds, using these to make sense of present conditions. The imaginary leads to ideological thinking, to contrasting present experiences with those of the remembered past, to providing individuals with understandings and beliefs by which they can live. The symbolic has its role also. It is the arena of speech and language that allows individuals to express differences and understandings. Word presentations shape the traditions and beliefs of a people, providing them with linguistic structures grounded in synonyms and antonyms, positives and negatives, beginnings and endings, and so forth. Through language, the world is made intelligible as a series of dialectical oppositions and resolutions.[2]

The person in the symbolic order becomes a divided self, a "me" and an "I." He is separated into a subject who acts and an object who is acted upon, who is referred to by others. Yet he is capable of understanding Otherness and the Other—he sees the world as a natural given and the order of human civilization as a social construct or imposition.

The imaginary and symbolic functions of humans help them to interpret social reality, giving it a history and rationale. An individual sees something and interprets it in words, failing to note the double misrecognition occurring in this transfer of images and symbols (the image is not the thing; the word is not the image or the thing).

It is not without intention that we speak of misrecognition or false consciousness. For the person is further removed from his social reality because of an ideological effect that situates and identifies him within a unified and cohesive cultural world. This ideological effect allows him to believe that he is knowledgeable about things he has never experienced or encountered, except in the imaginary realm of his consciousness. The imaginary provides the linkages that permit him to grasp his interpersonal family and world.

But what part does all this play in our understanding of schooling in capitalist systems? Only that the ideological effects of the family are continued and strengthened in the inculcation tasks of state schools. In accordance with the ideas and beliefs of society, we must regard the normative structures and pedagogic actions of teachers as acts of symbolic control and violence: the pedagogic act identifies and situates both teachers and students in a struggle for power and dominance in classrooms. In its pedagogic practices and arbitrary curriculum and habitus, this educational system resembles nothing more than a training ground for workers who must labor in incredibly rationalized and boring bureaucracies and factories in modern industry—that is to say, they must be taught to perform boring, meaningless work without being allowed to get up from their seats and leave the school (or workplace). The educational system, which is funded to teach youth the values of punctuality, cleanliness, good work habits, and a mindless acceptance of the social relations that exist in society, is itself an unconscious structure of the social system, whose history and meanings have been clouded by their need to perpetuate not only capitalist relations in the labor market but dominant and submissive relations in the schools and classrooms. Here we once again meet the evidences of misrecognition that seem to govern so much of the individual's life in mass society. Speech and language pour forth in the classroom as pedagogic efforts smash against the resistances of students; yet both teachers and students believe they are free in the actions they pursue and that their relationship is the fundamental one in the schooling experience. Seldom do they see or understand the unseen powers structuring and predetermining much of what happens to them in their work together; seldom do they see those interests served by pedagogic practices that affirm, again and again, the permanence and unity of modern capitalism and its production and distribution systems.

The Construction of the Pedagogic Situation

But what part is played by the imaginary and the symbolic in the schooling experiences of children and teachers? Only that both use imaginary and symbolic functions to provide initial suppositions about what classroom life will be like once their interaction begins. In accordance with these ideas, we can say again that the words of older siblings, parents, and friends help children to "know" their schools before they begin their schoolwork. The imaginary and symbolic functions permit the schooling situation to be conceptualized in advance, along with the kinds of behavior considered appropriate once children actually go to school. Children "know" whether a school is a good one or not, whether children fail or succeed there. Even in their earliest moments, they have ideas about what things will be like once they begin to study in their neighborhood school. The first behaviors of children are conditioned by these imaginary and symbolic constructs, which pass on to them the myths, traditions, and beliefs of state schools. Once they actually begin to interact with teachers and other students, they adjust their first impressions and behavior to fit the new realities of their situation. Here we can see the structural and relational principles that influence classroom life, helping students and teachers to make sense of schoolwork. Explanatory materials flow from these earlier suppositions, determining how students will respond to teachers' scolding and worse. Teachers and students use their knowledge of the situation to judge or explain away impositional actions and demands. Teachers may be given the benefit of the doubt in these circumstances, or students may come to identify them as overbearing, impositional taskmasters. Yet students can never really know how teachers will treat them until they attend classes themselves. Even then, knowledge is limited to their own experiences and their ability to interpret and integrate such experiences into their symbolic systems. The students' role will be described and explained, first by outsiders, and then by the teachers themselves. Often students' first experiences in state schools confirm their worst suppositions and govern their earliest responses.

Those who have studied the communication systems in classrooms have been impressed with their one-sidedness; it has seemed that students are acknowledged and ignored in the same moment, in the same discourse. They are acknowledged by the teacher's words, directed at them and meant to guide them in their deportment and studies. But they are ignored as individuals with personal identities and inclinations and expected to respond, en masse, to the demands of the teacher. In the classroom, youngsters discover that they are all students; they must listen and obey, accepting lower status and dependency without question or resistance. Students are able to grasp what teachers say by assuming their motives, by transferring memories and emotions from earlier situations. These are then refined to meet the realities of classroom experiences.

The value of the imaginary and the symbolic is in their creation of a learning situation that teachers and students consider normal, reasonable, and legitimate. Students come to accept that they will have to provide school staff members with proof of their right to be present at all times. If they are in the halls, they can be stopped and searched for appropriate passes; in classrooms, they must sit in assigned seats, respond to attendance checks, and place their coats on assigned hooks. In this way, legitimate members of the school can be differentiated from outsiders and intruders. The symbolic provides teachers with a means for determining who is and is not a teacher or student in the school. Teachers and students see the school building as the place where educational training properly takes place. Both accept the normative structures that view such training as serious and worthwhile communal efforts. The speech patterns of teachers define the dominant and subordinate roles and behaviors expected in classrooms. Students are individuals who need pedagogic guidance and work; they do not know what they need to learn in schools. Teachers, on the other hand, are surrogate parents or guardians, possessing great power over students in the schooling situation. Again and again, students and teachers experience classroom interactions in two ways: as suppositions about what they can expect to happen once classroom discourses begin, and as perceptions once the pedagogic action commences.

The interaction of the imaginary, the symbolic, and the real can best be understood by linking them to the mimetic structures and common cultural and linguistic heritages that have created state schools in mass society. These give the imaginary an opportunity to intersect with the ideological functions that veil the power behind pedagogical authorities; they allow for a maintenance of beliefs in an egalitarian school system even as the poorer classes fail generation after generation. Language permits students and teachers to understand each other by referring to a common stock of knowledge. From this, they are able to determine whether certain expected features of a learning situation are absent or present. Word presentations produce meanings through a never-ending chain of signification that links the present to the past. Teachers usually speak at children rather than to them, producing understandings that are completed by the imaginary functions of students.

Here is an example of an ordinary encounter taken from my visitation to an inner-city junior high school.

A youngster came toward me as I was talking to two teachers on hall duty.

"Excuse me," one of the teachers said. Then he turned in the direction of the approaching boy.

"You!" he said, gesturing toward the boy and motioning him closer.

"Yes," said the youngster.

"Show me your pass."

The boy searched his pockets but did not come up with any pass.

"You need a pass to be here," the teacher said in a stern voice.

"I had one . . ."

"But you don't have one now! What class are you supposed to be in? Who is your home-room teacher? Are you a student in this school? I don't remember seeing you before."

These words showed quite clearly the social status of teachers and students. No student would ever address a teacher by calling out, "You!" the way this teacher did. No student would use the gestures or tone of this overbearing but anxious teacher. The dialectical relationship between teachers and students was established in the first moments of the youngster's schooling. Language provided him with a clearer understanding of his subordinacy in the school, and the act of speech itself confirmed the status differences existing once he entered the building. Teachers and students are caught in a web of ideological effects and affiliations. Their relations are structured by normative understandings and traditions about what is supposed to occur in state classrooms. The content of schooling is important, but its practices are more important because they reaffirm the idea that authoritarianism is an acceptable and reasonable way to prepare youngsters for adult life in a democratic society. Schooling is concerned with the reproduction of the social relations existing in the schools and society, and its practices teach youngsters who the boss is, what the boss expects from his future workers, and so on. Students and teachers attempt to make sense of this world of schooling, but their efforts are hampered by distorted perceptions and the symbolic order of their culture. The external reality of the school is conveyed by the psychic reality of the Word and the imaginary functions of teachers and students.

The multiplicity of the reality of schooling can only be grasped by these imaginary and symbolic orders; it can only be understood by the interventions and words of others. These give the impression of an external reality that can be taken at face value. Teachers monitor the behavior and work habits of students and grade them accordingly, paying little conscious attention to linguistic and cultural heritages. The student's inability to respond has adverse consequences for him, no matter how attuned the teacher may be to his personal problems. This is the core element in the reality of pedagogic action. Another example may help us to see how these reactions to language can affect the teacher's view of her students. The teacher in this example began by complaining about her many problems, even though she taught kindergarten in an upper-middle-class suburban school in southern California. After some preliminary remarks, she got around to the source of her difficulties. Children were being bused from the nearby military base, she told me, raising her eyes in dismay; they were terribly ignorant and rowdy and not at all like the other children in her class.

"These children are different . . ."
"How?"
"Well, for one thing, they don't know their numbers and colors! They don't know the alphabet, and they simply won't sit still for very long."
"They're a problem?"
"A very big problem. They don't know any of the things they should know, if you know what I mean. Why, they don't even know they have a last name!"

This is where the symbolic and the real meet, where the suppositions of classroom life come together, revealing the prejudices and callousness of teachers. It is for the student to show that he knows what he ought to know before the work begins, that he is capable of mastering the materials. The fact is that poor preparation for schooling will not be corrected by classroom experiences in kindergarten or later in the primary grades. Also, incorrect answers or silences will not be tolerated; when the teacher's questions remain unanswered, it adds an unspoken Word to what has already gone before, continuing the chain of meaning and condemning students to a lifetime of failure in schools. The teacher confers her own meanings on the incorrect or passive responses of students, and these are recorded in grade books and discussed in teachers' lounges.

The teacher uses her words to construct the real world of the classroom; she also creates a sense of time in her charges, preaching the virtues of punctuality, hard work, competition, deferential deportment, and so on. Time is demanded of the student from his earliest years until he reaches young adulthood. Time is notable in the compulsory attendance laws that force youngsters to attend state schools long after logic would have dictated another course; it also marks the end of a student's schooling experience and his entrance into the labor market. We can predict with some certainty how well and how long children will attend schools, and we can trace their early and continued failures through the grade system.

A student's ability to master the language and culture of academia is probably in place before he ever enters the classroom. That is to say, he either has or does not have preschool experiences that will help him speak and understand the language and culture of schools. What are the implications of these insights for minority and poor children in the inner-city schools of the United States? There is no question that they have relevance. These children enter the schools with a native language other than English and a native culture that is very different from that of their educational systems. The tracking of these children begins the moment they enter their neighborhood schools, because the school itself is a track that leads to massive student failure. This can be confirmed by the scandalously high failure rates reported for minority children in all of the big cities of our nation.

Schooling's Alienating Effects

The impersonality of schooling in inner cities provides us with an extreme example of its alienating effects. Teachers use the ideology of education to justify impositional treatment of inner-city children, and the children themselves seem to accept such behaviors for their "own good." Both appear unaware of the true nature of their work together. Only when teachers fail to educate, and students fail to learn, do they perceive that problems exist. But the problems never focus on the hidden curriculum and agenda of the practices and goals of schooling nor the ideological effects that mask the unequal nature of student competition.

Teacher actions and opinions, as a rule, are enough to maintain the web of affiliations that ensnares students into the culture of the classroom. Pedagogic actions provide youngsters with "unintended" learnings that are not part of the official state curriculum. The Word of teachers provides youngsters with value judgments about themselves, their families, their cultural histories and primary languages, their race, and their sex. Such discourses also evaluate the students' progress through the grade system, providing them with a realistic appraisal of their chances for further education and success in the workplace. In fact, it is the teacher who uses speech and language to achieve the social and educational goals of schooling. Each day, she presents her view of the world, performing pedagogic actions that confuse and trouble students from different racial, ethnic, and linguistic backgrounds. She takes their passivity for ignorance, their anger and aggressiveness for a personal assault on her efforts and authority.

In these circumstances, regression is a normal response: the fantasies of the past provide some relief and guidance for the frustrations that students feel in their unequal relations with teachers. These regressions are not the clinical kind, as we have noted. They are more of an attempt to find safety and security in the infantile behaviors of an earlier period when parents also dominated every bodily movement and thought of children. Their current relations with teachers and peers are so disturbing that they must either adapt to their institutional roles, withdraw into themselves, or lash out at the offending parties.

Thus, the educational experiences of teachers and students can be very misleading for both groups; the effects of the Word may be understood, but the emotional force behind the words may be hidden from view. The rules of classroom life exclude real contact between teachers and students, forcing both to attend to the pedagogic work that separates them further. Teachers who believe otherwise might retrace their own experiences as students and student-teachers. Seldom, if ever, were they able to grasp the real situation or relationship developing between them and their mentors. Perhaps they will also remember that the real was never accessed in their schoolwork either: the teacher or supervisor performed her work by constant surveillance and by judging students in a competitive ethos. She supervised every movement in the room, checking to see if students were doing their work in the prescribed manner. And the student-teacher or teacher who searches her memory may remember as well how she withdrew her emotions and personal identity from the classroom situation, how she de-emphasized schoolwork so that she could overcome the more impersonal institutional identity of the unknowing and irresponsible student (or student-teacher). In this apprenticeship, teachers learned to teach as they were taught, relying on traditional authority that persists, even though legal-rational authority has supplanted traditionalism in mass, bureaucratic schools.

Thus, the student or student-teacher acts as a reproductive relay, as do all students. He assures the reproduction and continuity of the social relations of educational production and, through this, those relations that prevail in the social and economic system of adults. Teachers internalize the pedagogic and authoritarian beliefs of the educational system first, coming to see things through the eyes of the veteran teachers and administrators who preceded them.

The results are a series of practices and social structures that regiment students much as military and penal colonies do. A punishment-oriented, corrective ethos has been established and maintained for many centuries and can be seen in classrooms today. Methods for distributing children, locating them in special areas or classrooms, sorting them in ability groups, evaluating their performances and recording them in cumulative files, and forcing them to interact where they could be easily observed and controlled were all features of penal and military communities centuries ago. The practices of forcing children to respond to commands predate modern organizational forms; the desire of those in authority positions to create obedient, responsive students by constraining their bodily movements has its roots in the prehistory of the human condition.

Discipline in our present-day schools is still defined by a student's right to be present in a particular place in the school building. An individual's age and place in the organization is the determining factor in deciding who speaks and who listens, who orders and who obeys. Discipline is merely one way that rank is affirmed and strengthened. It designates the authority of adults: they are the ones who assign places to students, routinizing and regimenting schoolwork. Supervision, as we have noted, has become a simple matter of noticing whether youngsters are deviating in some way from the prescribed behaviors and work habits of the teacher.

Paradoxically, this simulation of the work environment has had unintended effects. Personal relationships have become so affected by repressed emotions that schools often fail to accomplish their minimal goals. Teaching has become more than a mere recitation and evaluation of rote and arbitrary curricula; the grading and selecting of successful and unsuccessful children has become an important end in itself. It is necessary to coerce children to be attentive to meaningless work without questioning its efficacy. Observers have been quick to note the consequences: teachers have become little more than drill masters, preparing children for tests, and children have become less human and involved and more robotized. The schoolwork has become unbearably boring and meaningless to students, and their deportment has become more suitable for a factory, office, or military camp than an educational institution. Teachers have sought obedience from students, yet it has subverted thinking and inquiry. Students take their places quietly and sit through lessons without involving themselves or being properly prepared.

If the teacher could remember her own schooling experiences in these repressive educational systems, she might loosen her control a bit. The greatest advantage she could derive from her situation would be to place herself in her students' positions, imagining their feelings toward her and classroom life. Then she could begin to deal with the reality that lies beneath the formal behavior of students. She might listen to their words, understanding that she could learn much from them. If this were to actually happen, students would surely raise questions about what they were learning, why the lessons were so boring, and why the discipline was so encompassing.

Without this two-way communication, the teacher must fall back on her imaginary relationships with students. She will then be forced to fill in the blanks when children come to school unprepared, late, or absent. By assuming the all-knowing, always-talking teacher role, she will shut her students out of classroom discourses, closing down open communication between them.

She will not be able to hear her students' frustrations and confusions; she will not know how her efforts are being experienced by the children she is supposed to serve. For she has no other way of learning what is happening in her classroom than through this open, two-way discourse. And such discourse is impossible as long as she is the "boss," the dictator of all decisions made in her room.

Students will speak in empty words when they are called upon to recite in these penal-like settings. Their desires, aspirations, hopes, and fears will never come to the surface; they will never commit themselves to the classroom experiences that dominate and control them. Their words will have less and less value for them and for their teacher. Too many of the individual psychological factors of the reality of the classroom are missing from such encounters. Teachers may believe that their role is to modify the individual behavior and character of students, but such actions force children to defend themselves against the hidden message of rejection contained in such communications: you are not good enough as you are—if you were, it would not be necessary to change you.

If we now turn to the history of schooling, we will see that the value of educational training has always been determined by adults. Opposed to the untrained and undisciplined minds of children they have placed the military discipline of encampment and the workplace. Against the resistances of children, the state and its agents have put in place a symbolic structure that interprets schooling in ideological cadences.

Discipline in the mass school is a form of power that uses an entire array of methods, procedures, levels of application, and so on. It is a technology concerned with correction and control, with teaching children through constant discourse who they are and what they can expect in the social and economic world of adults. And it is exercised by teachers who are responsible for reintegrating the power and authority of educators during the schooling process.

Discipline is the art of surveillance. Behind the appearance of classroom decorum, the teacher searches for the uniform behavior and responses of students; behind the demands for standardized responses and learnings, there is the need to train youth who will be useful in capitalist society. The execution of disciplinary actions reinforces the power and status of those who have been legally sanctioned to operate our educational system.

A capitalist society obsessed with punctuality, competition, order, and predictability is the consequence of historical forces that go back several centuries. In schools, and other bureaucratic and corporate structures, similar methods are used to insure the continuation of the social status system. This phenomena of reproduction can be observed in every society known to us: every system is confronted with the problem of maintaining and sustaining itself. But the modern mass school uses disciplinary methods to achieve five specific functions: (1) to obtain control and power over students by referring to commonly held values and beliefs that are part of America's social heritage; (2) to reduce resistance to decreasing visibility of schools through the use of separate buildings, classrooms, and detention centers that are partitioned off from the surrounding communities; (3) to maximize the effects of their authority and power by using them throughout the school day; (4) to justify this coercion and control over the student's body and mind by linking such practices to the outcomes of educational agencies; and (5) to increase the usefulness and docility of students so that they can perform more effectively in the mechanistic world of work without questioning the power structures they encounter there. These aims of school discipline coincide with those of business and industry. One consequence of the Industrial Revolution was the enormous rise in the number of people on Earth. This population tended to move about more, thereby thwarting the aims of those who sought to keep them in their places so that they could be managed and controlled. A change of this magnitude forced legal-rational educational agencies to imitate the disciplinary practices of military, religious, and penal institutions. By the middle of the twentieth century, billions of people were counted in the world's population. This was also associated with worldwide problems of productivity and economic distribution and the development of bureaucratic systems that trained workers not to walk away from increasingly rationalized, boring work. The development of disciplinary systems is no doubt linked to these new conditions and the rise of bureaucratic authority and society. Legal-rational power was built into the organizational structures of modern institutions so that they could vastly increase the productivity and manageability of workers.

A Struggle for Dominance

The first thing that becomes clear to anyone studying classroom life is that a struggle for dominance and power exists between teachers and students. Conflicts are ongoing, persistent, and less onerous than those occurring in the workplace. Yet the dominant submissive relationship of the classroom has its roots in the precapitalist period and earlier, when the master-slave role set was more easily visible.[3]

The child represses his social needs and desires in the classroom because he has accepted the imaginary ideas (or ideologies) of education: it is a serious and important enterprise deserving his attendance and respect. He accepts his subordinacy and regimentation because all of his own kith and kin have advised him to do so, and because of his own dependent status in his family and communal relations. Yet on another level, there is an unconscious conflict and struggle for supremacy between teachers and students, and teachers are quite aware of it.[4] The child can never accept his institutional identity and the negation of his personal self; he must, on some level, always struggle against the conscious and reasonable arguments of adults. Relationships in the symbolic order may speak about unified efforts to achieve common goals, but the reality of the struggle for dominance in classrooms is a constant negation of such ideological pronouncements. Teachers try to exercise symbolic control over students, and youngsters defend themselves as best they can. The danger point may occur when children decide that they have nothing to gain by integrating themselves into the coercive educational environments of mass schools; without the consent of students, no pedagogic situations can be constructed by educators. Teachers have the decisional rights over students, but only so long as children are willing to concede these rights.

The ability to force youngsters to move on command and do schoolwork is only too well documented in the educational literature, but its psychological and educational consequences are universally ignored. Children are filled with ambivalence toward their adult mentors; they have repressed animosities that are often hidden from teachers. (Any rights they may have had to control their bodily movements and thoughts are given up once they enter the school.) But they sense that the teacher's authority rests on a fragile social compact and that such agreements can come apart. As long as students accept schooling as a legitimate and worthwhile activity and renounce their own desires and needs, the authority of teachers is secure. But when years of failure erode children's acceptance of the pedagogic discipline, they usually act up and drop out.

Until this happens, schoolwork follows the dictates and intentions of teachers, further alienating students from themselves and their education. For not only is the learning decided by the teacher—mimicking the dominant-submissive relationships of traditional schools and workplaces—but the students' achievements are often short term and meaningless to them. They cannot see themselves or their life experiences in the pedagogic efforts of state schools. They wait for passage through the grade system to end so that they can begin to live their lives again. But they also identify with teachers in an ambivalent way, and as a result, they are often cajoled into accepting the negative roles of their educational identities.

Still, students seek to deceive their taskmasters by feigning interest while doing as little as possible to get by. Here the ego seeks to silence the demands of the superego as best it can. To gain favor with the mercurial, all-powerful pedagogue, the pupil performs his schoolwork and submits to the constant evaluation and correction of his thoughts and movements. It is his way of partially disarming his tormentor. From the moment class work begins, both teachers and students seek to defuse the fears and anxieties of the other. And students never tire of assuring teachers that they are harmless and pose no threat to their power and authority.

It is not surprising, then, that many teachers speak disdainfully of students when they are alone with one another. They disparage their educational achievements, even when these are on or above grade level. But their severest barbs are reserved for the millions of inner-city and minority children from different cultural and linguistic backgrounds. The children's resistance and response to these attitudes can be observed in their failure to do anything more than what is absolutely required of them.

Here we are at the hub of the controversy that Willard Waller spoke about many years ago. In the struggle to force youngsters to learn mandated curricula, language, and social status, the seeds of constant conflict are sown. If teachers would allow children to learn what was of interest to them, very little conflict would take place in public-school classrooms. The Word would then be used to explore the complexities of the student's world, and his personal identity could be preserved. But since this cannot be in state schools, there is nothing but resistance and repression, even in the segregated, suburban schools. Does this mean that educational systems are failing in their mission? Of course not; they achieve their functions of inculcation even if teachers are unaware of what they are actually doing in classrooms. They prepare youngsters to adapt to the boss-worker dichotomy of the workplace by forcing them to accept the unequal relationships that exist in state schools and classrooms.

Pedagogic action achieves its effects in the imaginary and symbolic structures it creates in the minds of teachers and students. These lie at the center of the social identities developed in school and later in the labor market. Such identities are institutional, structured in negativity through a tradition of unconscious understandings that predate the modern period. They permit teachers and students to recognize one another, while misrecognizing the true nature of their socially constructed classroom situations. In the beginning, there are open resistances, and the child seeks to return to his personal identity and familial associations in a nostalgia for the nurturing environment and Other. Later he comes to accept his student identity and the others in his classroom, but this often takes time. Now he finds himself one of many, competing for recognition in an impersonal, standardized setting. He transfers emotions and understandings from his past onto his teachers and classmates and is unaware of the countertransference that often occurs. It is only in the early primary grades that the full force of the effects of schooling begin to be felt as a negative, rejecting, and unsatisfying experience.

The student in these early grades has a desire to be recognized as a separate, unique person. He seeks recognition not as a group member but as an individual. He seeks to rediscover himself in the group activities of pedagogy and withdraws once he becomes frustrated and confused by classroom practices. He becomes conscious of himself through the recognition he receives from teachers and students. He learns that his consciousness is really self-consciousness and that this exists within himself. It is merely a reflection transmitted in language and in his own imaginary order. He can only exist if the teacher recognizes him in a dialectic of dominance and submission, if she permits him to stand, get out of his seat, or speak.

The imaginary in classroom life refers to the relations that shape a student's self-image over time. The symbolic introduces the entire world of schooling and pedagogy to the thought and language processes of the child. Words designate things in the classroom, allowing teachers and students to see the environment as a self-evident and unchangeable given. In pedagogic actions, the transference occurs through the person of the dominant adult, since she has the actual power and authority in the classroom. She interprets the student's words and behavior by constantly evaluating and grading them.

When we speak of the relations between teachers and students, we have in mind one thing: the power and authority teachers have over every movement and thought of children in schools. We cannot put it any other way. These outcomes of pedagogic action lead to the symbolic controls and violence about which European scholars have spoken and to the serious misrecognitions of the schooling situation by participants. Teachers routinely refuse to acknowledge the role they play in the failures and frustrations of their students; they do not want to face their complicity in the poorly schooled students who have dropped out and who educational authorities have labelled as failures. They use the Word to stratify knowledge and the speech and cultural backgrounds of students to stratify the children themselves. They use the printed Word to deny school failures the opportunity to progress further in education or to vie for the more important and desirable jobs in the labor market. Grading practices unite and divide teachers and students in the same moment; students need the good will of teachers if they are to progress through the system, even as pedagogues tend to destroy open communications and the educational experience. Students come to mistrust teachers even as they need recognition and acceptance from them. And teachers use their grading power to control the behavior of their charges even as they seek their love and acceptance.

In summary, repressive defenses are a natural consequence of the attack on the self accompanying pedagogic actions in state schools. The children have the experiences of the Oedipal adjustment to guide them as they deal with this new, powerful adult and the threat she poses to their normal desires and needs for recognition. A student may want to strike out at his teacher in order to be rid of her and the onerous experience of schooling, much as he wished his father out of the way or dead. He must protect himself; he must defend against the daily humiliations of classroom life. He must do so while trying to fit into the pedagogical system and symbolic controls of educational authorities. He cannot reject his educational experiences without drawing upon himself the opprobrium of parents and teachers. He cannot condemn pedagogic practices because they are supported by the myths, traditions, and ideologies of modern capitalist states. He cannot disavow education (he does not want to learn what every adult tells him he should learn, his parents will be disgraced if he fails or drops out of school, and so on). His withdrawal from the educational system would simply validate the mandate and function of schooling in mass society: sort out and stratify students so that they can be prepared for places in the educational and socioeconomic pyramid.

In regard to the reasons for student attendance, we need only to consult the compulsory attendance laws and the demands and acquiescences of parents and other "good folk." The child is used to free movement and a reasonably open expression of his aggressive and sexual feelings in his home environment. Before he enters school, he has learned to differentiate himself from others; he has become a "me" who exists as a separate person and an "I" who acts upon his environment to achieve his desires. But once he enters the state school, his teacher gains the right and duty to control his bodily movements and gestures;

she is the one who can force him to "sit still" and "be silent"; she can punish and humiliate him with a word when he acts out aggressive or sexual feelings. He is still a "me" in the classroom. He can still be referred to as an individual member of the classroom group. But he is extremely limited in the amount of time he can act as an "I," changing his classroom environment to suit his own needs and desires. The teacher now takes the place of the symbolic father, even when she is a woman. This symbolic Other differs from the imaginary and real father of the child because she (or he) functions only during the school day.

The teacher is related to her students by a dialectic of dominance and submission, aggressiveness and passivity. She is the only important signifier in the room, the only one who can say what is to be done or what is being done in her domain. She is a singular presence who commands the attention of her students while recognizing them only in their institutional roles. Education derives its power from these coercive practices and from the students' willingness to accept and internalize them: they are for the students' "own good." The language relationship between teachers and students, with no interlocutor between them, almost always results in one-sided discourses and evaluations. She tells her charges what the learning situation is, and why she is ethically bound to force them to attend to it. By the very fact of her singularity, by her constant talking and commanding, she imposes her will through continuous discourse.

Even if the work is meaningless for the student, even if he is powerless to change his condition in the classroom, he may not say what is on his mind—he may not say what he means. Thus, the relations between teachers and students are established through a series of closed communications. The student seeks to turn the teacher into a substitute parent through a transference of previous thoughts, feelings, and behaviors. He gives this new dominant adult the attributes of others whom he has known in the past. Unconsciously, he substitutes these older images for the teacher who stands before him, determining his behavior by reenacting actions and attitudes that worked well for him in these previous relationships. While this occurs, the teacher also uses a countertransference to govern her reactions to students. Their relations are individual to individual, even though the students' behaviors are always seen as part of a group phenomena. Students cannot recognize these unconscious defenses that they erect, and teachers are often unable to take the place of the other and understand how the children really feel about things. Teachers are also unaware of their prejudices toward children from different social and ethnic backgrounds, preferring to believe that they "treat all of their children the same."

There can be no doubt that the teacher-pupil relationship is an unconscious one, molded in constant discourse and a cumulative written file. Both engage in classroom interaction without being aware of the power of others who are not in the classroom or who have lived long ago. This misrecognition of the political sources of their behavior is compounded by the work that goes on between them. Such work is determined by the symbolic order that they share and the social structures that were created in the past and now act on them as though they were independent, immutable forces. The imaginary order perceives the bounded order of the classroom; it sees images and is separate from the symbolic order and the real, which it seeks to apprehend. But it allows teachers and students to believe that they are at the center of the teaching/learning process. In schools, teachers and students discover their social selves and class positions in society. From the beginning, they learn to perceive and internalize their relationships to others. These powerful social identifications mark students and teachers alike, but it is with the students that the school's inculcation function is most concerned.

Finally, the development of the student's institutional identity is a critical aspect in the formation of his class position in capitalist society. Schooling is a centering, limiting experience for children, taming their animal natures and preparing them to accept a life of labor. Communication is the central feature of schooling; the symbolic order creates a world of words, permitting participants to make sense of classroom life. Language, as we have noted earlier, is an intersubjective phenomena, separate and apart from those individuals who use it to speak and communicate. It is something known and available to teachers and students in the most favorable situations. It acquires a social dimension when the mimetic structures created by the language of individuals in the past also interact with teachers and students, presenting them as social realities that exist apart from the will of present-day persons. Thus, the many-sided relationships between signifier and signified are complicated by ideological apparatuses that the state uses to protect its interests.

The symbolic order is different from the traditional schooling structures that exist today and affect the lives of so many people. Common-sense meanings of words mask the unconscious processes that precede all speech; the ambiguity of communications is eased by the imaginary and by clarifying statements that seek to grasp the meaning of the real world. The social structures of society can be seen as those forces that determine where and how schooling will be experienced, while the speech and behavior of participants represent attempts to exert their free will within the limited horizons of state schools.

7

Problems and Possibilities

Any theory encompassing the subjective and objective aspects of human life will encounter obvious problems. The theories of Marx and Freud differ in their selection of subjective or objective criteria as their focus of study. Yet both found common ground in their belief that man's ability to know himself and his social reality was limited. We need not infer a complete correspondence between these master theories, but recent work in linguistics and structural Marxism has given hope for a synthesis, even as serious difficulties remain. Freudians speak of the unconscious and the inner world of impulses and desires, while Marx wrote about ideology and the false consciousness it creates for classes in conflict. Nevertheless, both used rational thought (and language) to apprehend the psychological and social realities of their times.

The basic tenets held by psychoanalysts are not couched in the phrases of historical materialism and class theory, two essential features of Marxist thought. Even so, Lacanianism introduced language into the study of these socialization and inculcation processes, while Louis Althusser used symbolic processes to situate the individual in structural Marxist theory. Since psychoanalysts have based their theories on observations of individuals in bourgeois society, an obvious problem presents itself: while Freudians believe that the familial complexes that determine the development of human personality in capitalist society are true for all ages and social systems, Marxists hold that the identity of the individual is primarily a function of his historical class position.

Without attempting any exhaustive enumeration, we may point to certain unities to which these theories tend. The mind, both assume, cannot experience itself or its world directly, requiring reflection and symbolic functions to give it an imaginary order and purpose. But since this can only be done through images and language, the real can never be experienced except as representations. The question arises whether the thoughts and language of the individual are completely his, or whether they are those of others who have lived in the past and taught him his place in the symbolic order. Moreover, there is no possibility of ignoring the central place of the unconscious in Freudian thought, along with its emphasis on a conflict-ridden, irrational, erotic, and aggressive nature. The unconscious offers a world hidden from casual awareness and understanding even when we are consciously seeking to uncover its secrets. While we are awake or sleeping, the unconscious controls speech and language and is the repository of a repressed and forgotten past, distorting our self-images and view of the world.

Marx also believed that illusions and ideology distorted the self-perceptions of individuals, alienating them from their own best interests. The controlling ideas of a given period always had the closest affinity to the dominant classes of society; their general acceptance or rejection was determined by the class structure and social order. Lacanianism used the concepts of the imaginary and symbolic to explain how individuals found their places in families and social hierarchies, internalizing the myths, traditions, and language of their people (and classes). In terms of the imaginary and the ideological, both theories tended toward a view that rationalizing human thinking masked the true interests of individuals living in bourgeois society.

This skepticism about the common-sense understanding and nature of everyday life is a recurring theme in both theories. Marx believed that a higher consciousness would strip away the ideological effects of bourgeois society, helping the proletariat to see the true nature of their oppressed condition; Freud thought that a knowledge of repressed psychic phenomena would free his patients from their neurotic symptoms. Of course Marxism sought to provide the masses with an understanding of their conditions and a way out of them, thus crossing the line into ideology itself! But Marx's questions and methods of research provided a deep and lasting glimpse into the essential features of modern capitalism. His use of successive approximations, starting with the worker-capitalist relationship, showed that knowledge of the social and economic world would need constant and renewed study.

The theory in which primarily the individual is important is psychoanalysis; little attention is paid to important persons or institutions that existed in the past. The only history that Freud was interested in was that of his patients or of important individuals who lived in the past. Structural Marxists and psychoanalysts have tended to pay little more than lip service to the history of their decentered subjects, but this is not an inherent defect of their system. It would be easy to show how history and social relations could be given a specificity and place, especially if we abandoned the notion that the symbolic alone determines human personality. The symbolic order is the given that determines the parameters of an individual's life and contacts, but he still possesses genetic and linguistic abilities, selecting and reacting to new situations differently from his forebears and from deterministic predictions. The application to a comprehensive theory of social life is strengthened by Marx's theories of false consciousness and the unconscious of Freudianism. A knowledge of these hidden processes permits men and women to grow in insight and understanding, making them better able to respond to the realities of their lives. For Freud, there was a tendency to believe men had an essential, biological anchor to their natures that was unchangeable and separated from the social identities they were forced to play in their property relations with one another. Marx, on the other hand, believed that human personality and behavior were decisively influenced by a person's class position in the competitive ethos of modern capitalism.

The application of psychoanalysis to Marxist theory can fill an important blank space: it alludes to the etiology of human nature and thought missing in Marxist literature. For objective theories of the human condition often omit consideration of how the individual is created. How does he come to think and speak as he does? Where does his identity come from, and why is he so easily taken in by ideological effects? Here psychoanalysis, as we have seen, provides a bridge; the symbolic and imaginary orders furnish mechanisms that the individual can use to apprehend and reflect upon social reality. And this can be done within the context of documented, clinical findings about human nature as it has evolved in the nineteenth and twentieth centuries.

This view of psychoanalysis would be incomplete if we did not mention that, by and large, theories of neurotic and normal behaviors were not linked to capitalism and the social relations of production. Still, Marxists appear to have been proven wrong in their ideas about Freudianism and the nature of human nature. A synthesis that could integrate the subjective and objective aspects of the social life of individuals in capitalist society has floundered over the complexities of the sociohistorical influences and the mysteries of the unconscious. Yet the contradictory aspects of these two systems can be eased by greater attention and research into the linguistic and cultural features of contemporary life. Certain contradictions may persist even after these ideas have been taken to more significant levels of analysis. The individual as subject needs to be reconciled to the deterministic ideas of Marxism; the conflict between the individual's psychic needs and the demands of society require further study and synthesis.

Those who cannot accept the obvious contradictions between the subjective forms of psychoanalysis and the societal focus of Marxism will find themselves dissatisfied with attempts to link the two. But there are commonalities between these disciplines: both sought to look beneath the surface of psychic and societal appearances in order to understand hidden essences and etiologies. Both were rooted in materialism, believing that the sources behind appearances were hidden from the casual consciousness of individuals and needed to be exposed through scientific, rational analysis. Marx saw capitalism as a contradictory, oppressive system in which the interests of workers and those of capital necessarily came into conflict. Through constant study, the past could be understood and the future predicted. Freud, on the other hand, saw that man's instinctual nature was charged with unconscious, libidinal energies and discord. What mattered was a scientific study of these psychic structures to provide individuals with greater consciousness and insight into their true natures. Both believed that human lives were determined by social and psychic phenomena that had occurred in the past, but they also believed that within the parameters set by such determinations, free choice was possible.

The mental and social world of humans was not easily comprehensible, in either view. People are not in control of their consciousness nor of the social relations of production that shape their lives. Freud's emphasis on erotic and aggressive drives, however, seems quite different from Marx's focus on the class dynamics and social history of individuals and peoples. Yet these need not be unsurmountable obstacles to any synthesis, especially when the voice of the Other and Otherness provide symbolic and cultural linkages between the systems. Relations between sexuality and the class structure of society may prove to be one area where the two systems cannot come together easily. Still, there is enough commonality to warrant further study and research.

The application of man's nature (his animalism, egotism, aggressiveness, and essential amorality) to social planning and reform has the weight of clinical observations behind it. Yet Freudians and Marxists believe that reason can tame these impulsive, oppressive forces in human life. Marx's analysis of surplus value and capitalist forms of exploitation and alienation evolved from his classic studies of nineteenth-century capitalism, but they have their insistent echo today.

Freud's view of truth as a perilous journey inward through the uncharted pathways of the mind is no doubt a landmark achievement in the development of human thought. Marx, on the other hand, looked outward and saw the inequities of the class conflicts that have existed since the beginning of recorded history. But Freud was right when he noted an intense religiosity and fervor associated with the supposedly scientific arguments of latter-day Marxists.

So the questions remain: Can psychoanalysis be used to

deepen our understanding of historical materialism? Can Marxism inform psychoanalysis, forcing it to pay closer attention to the historical contexts and class positions of its patients? Freudianism can help us to understand the cultural class struggle that rages beneath the surface of such ideological state apparatuses as the family, schools, churches, the media, political parties, and so on. Marxism can provide insights into the class war and the interests of people living and working in capitalist systems. Language, the indispensable link between thought and expression, can be used to bring these ideas together. Rather than focusing on the segregation and partition of social reality that characterizes the social sciences today, we should seek interdisciplinary theories that explain the subjective and objective experiences of people living and working in mass societies.

Applications

The applications of these theoretical constructs to education is the task of the next century. They allude to the etiology of schooling: the imaginary propensities of the mind lead to ideological effects, but only after the symbolic and social structures of the past have made themselves felt. Classroom life is made possible by a coordination of all these modes of thought and expression. They provide participants, in the first instance, with social structures from the past that must be attended to once the school day begins. The learning situation itself is constructed in words, words representing practices that existed and exist in present-day classrooms. But these word presentations are not the practices themselves; failing to see this is a major source of misrecognition, as Pierre Bourdieu showed in his formal theoretical work. Words gain their meaning from the differences that occur when one is chosen and its antonym is not. Teachers and students are ideological subjects gaining identity and roles from the imaginary relations and historical traditions of the past. It is in the mythology and folklore of schooling that the ideology of state education finds its validation. The classroom situation allows participants to identify one another as legitimate members and to assume that they are engaged in a common educational effort. This perspective unifies teachers and students at the same time as the state's inculcation requirement and police-like practices push them apart.

It is the uniformity and class bias of state schools that give them their depressing cast. Authority relies upon ideology to gloss over the contradictions associated with the dictates of the state and the obvious needs of individual students (and teachers). Differences are ignored or penalized, and teachers and students are forced to work in a corrective, coercive milieu. Even as officials speak of homogeneity and assimilation as their rationale for rejecting the race, ethnicity, sex, language, and familial heritages of minority and working-class children, the practices of social, age, and intellectual segregation undermine the democratic effects of schooling.

In mass schools, children are or are not taught the language and culture that they will need in the better schools and occupations of society: the determining variable is most often the race, sex, and class of students. Moreover, the unconscious features of human discourse structure the ideologies that unify teachers and students, undermining the learning experience by ignoring the sexual and recognitional needs of youngsters (and teachers). Pedagogy begins with an imaginary order of education, then moves into the symbolic discourse of actual practice. The latter leads to the dialectical relations that exist between teachers and students: word presentations reinforce the inequalities in their relationship. The act of speaking signifies who is in command; the act of listening and attending signifies who must submit.

The imaginary allows teachers and students to remain in opposition even as their work together speaks of unity and common purposes. Their work operates in the symbolic world of words, myths, and traditions—that is, in the world of the unconscious. The ideology of the business classes dominates the arbitrary curricula and practices of teachers, as does its ideas about race, ethnicity, sex, and class. In many inner-city classrooms, teachers and students are paralyzed by the contradictions of their schoolwork; they are unable to investigate those forces that dictate the content and practices they endure in mass schools. Very little interest is paid to what is taught in these inner-city schools: most time is spent maintaining order and keeping the children busy. The significance of these caretaker institutions is often ignored by teachers, who tend to see any purposeful work as useful. The imaginary and symbolic come together here, reaffirming the traditions and folklore of schooling the poor, of attacking their self-images and concepts. Teachers shift the problem from their failure to educate to educators' attitudes toward youngsters who come from poor and "disadvantaged" backgrounds.

Fetishism, Signifying, and the Specular

Three concepts seem important in understanding the actual classroom experiences of teachers and students. The Freudian idea of fetishism—as applied to all participants who are fixed in organizational roles by the reality of the image, language, and culture of their educational system—needs consideration first. Through fetishism, teachers and students are placed in a condition in which they find only imaginary coherences; they come together to justify common educational efforts, even when these lead to unintended and undesired outcomes. These are caused by their ignorance of the structure within which educational knowledge is produced and their true positions in the capitalist hierarchy.

A second significant concept is that of the signifier and the signified, in which teachers and students become effects for one another. They are substituted in the language each employs to navigate classroom relations; teachers and students are reduced to objects for one another, discussing each other as though they were things. The gaps in communication cause each to use inferences to make sense of everyday discourses. They must constantly reinvent themselves, reproducing appropriate behaviors in their institutional roles again and again. Without the signifier, or teacher, there would be no learning situation, no teacher or student. Ideology and the imaginary operate through these effects, and through their constant repetition. In inner-city classrooms, we can see that while the learning situation is a process of inculcation and production (a movement through which students must pass by law), the imaginary and ideological tie participants into this situation as an "I" and a "they," a "he" or a "she," as members who are engaged in a serious and important social purpose in democratic society. In the ebb and flow of activities, in its emphasis on academics and drill, in the endless corrections and evaluations, the classroom reproduces the uneven and arbitrary environment of the workplace, binding the student to the culture of capitalism. This is achieved through constant discourse at home and in school, and through other ideological structures in society.

A final important concept is that of the mirror stage, taken from the work of Henri Wallon and Jacques Lacan. In schools, there is the long arduous process of acculturation and inculcation; images of the student and his self are placed in conflict and find expression in academic achievements and failures, in adaptations. The educational experience creates a world in which the child's ego needs to be on constant guard, adapting to the demands of invisible forces and the arbitrary, mercurial teacher.

The reader may want to ask whether these perspectives provide an adequate, theoretical approach to the ideology, culture, and symbolic world of schooling in mass society. The focus on how students are subjected to inculcation through many years of pedagogic effort seems too limited an area of concern, even when it is linked to ideological effects and the base structure of Marxian theory. In capitalist states, in advanced technological societies, the boredom and routine of classroom life can be connected to the nature of work in mass society. The imaginary effects of schooling yield to a constant demand for passivity and deference; they force an anonymous student identity on children. The ideology of schooling puts youngsters in a position of pseudosubmissiveness, while placing teachers themselves in aggressive, impositional postures certified by the state. The give-and-take of the classroom becomes a reaffirmation of the status differences between children and adults. Pedagogy is always the arbitrary presentation of knowledge couched in the nuances of the shared symbolic order. It is always a particular point of view in which images and language are used to construct an intelligible world where student conversion and submission is required. The student is separated from himself and forced to adapt to the expected behavior and identity of his classroom role. He is fixed in this position by the language and culture of his family and by the state that forces him to attend public schools. But these symbolic and coercive forces are also supported by normative structures and ideological understandings of his people and the dominant classes in society.

The student is therefore reduced to a formal identity and set loose in mass schools. He soon learns that he is an anonymous other to his teachers even as his imaginary order constructs more hopeful and benign interpretations of classroom life. But this focus on the teacher-student relationship would be remiss if we failed to point out its ahistorical character. Both teachers and students are often unaware and unconcerned about the past and the ways in which it structures their current schoolwork. The nineteenth-century schools are forgotten, and traditional practices and disciplines are accepted as natural and common-sense ways of doing things. For educational systems, ideology is reality, and the tasks of assimilation, inculcation, and correction are never ending, requiring authoritarian approaches. To move away from traditional forms of competitive, class-biased education, it is necessary to have alternatives, and in capitalist systems, such alternatives simply do not exist. The student (and teacher) must retain ideological fixities if schools and the economic system are to survive, otherwise the entire hierarchical structure might collapse. A world of questioning, of recognizing differences and class interests, would undermine the social relations of the workplace, threatening capitalist institutions. There seems to be no way of effectively distancing ourselves from the symbolic controls and violence of pedagogic action, no way of discovering the sources of classroom conflicts and communications.

The drill and discipline of classroom life lead to boredom and fatigue. Humor is conspicuously absent from pedagogic work, and all knowledge and history are reduced to memorized "sound bites" that can be useful on standardized tests. The only acceptable behavior for students is to defer to and accept their teacher's unquestioned authority in the classroom. For current pedagogues, schooling is a serious and humorless affair in which educational knowledge is passed on to the young; it is not something to amuse or entertain them. The spirit of inquiry is an ideological construct masking the blind acceptance of traditional authoritarian methods in classroom life.

Historical Perspectives and Pedagogic Practices

From this we conclude that schooling must be understood within the context of historical materialism. The life of teachers and students today is the outcome of schooling and economic conditions as they existed at the end of the nineteenth century and earlier. The view of students as ignorant and unworthy persons has its roots in the charity schools of the early 1800s and the reform schools built for Irish truants in 1849. Schools constructed student images that fit their status and class positions in society. But subjugation was and is the condition of children even when their educational attainments are high. All students represent a captive, passive audience that cannot speak or move until told to do so. The arbitrary curriculum is not equally understandable or available to students; their race, ethnicity, sex, primary language, and health care all conspire to make the equal competition of educational knowledge less equal than it appears to be. The relations set up by classroom teachers bind children to an educational effort on their own behalf. They are to seek education and enlightenment, to make something of themselves now and in the future. The contradictions between the ideology of democracy and the realities of their class positions are never analyzed. Public education can be shown to have democratic value only if it can lift working-class and minority children out of their exploited and disadvantaged positions. And this it has not been able to do. Students are forced to attend neighborhood schools, causing them to learn in racially and economically segregated classrooms. The contradictions of such schooling have their causes in the demands of state schools and pedagogues and the differences between the language and culture of students and academia. The effects of class position play themselves out in the number of children who eventually attend the best colleges, medical schools, and so on, and those who must settle for the lesser schools and occupations in mass society. The reception of the official pedagogy of state schools varies with the differences that exist between them and the students they teach.

The student exists only in his school; he is constructed by the educational discourses of adults and forced to accept them. These have an imaginary component to them but are played out in the daily give-and-take of classroom life. The real world is only what is real for teachers and students working together in enclosed classrooms. The history and state laws and policies structuring pedagogic work are beyond the knowledge and understanding of most teachers and students.

From these observations, we can see that it is impossible for state schools to invite active, inquiring behavior from students. Their rationale is corrective, coercive, and oriented toward inculcation and reproduction. They are antidemocratic in history and practice, stripping students of inalienable rights to move or speak freely. Linguistic productions, and the social structures they created in the past, interact in the present, affecting the kind of social relations that develop in classrooms and workplaces. Schools show no interest in working-class children, preferring to treat all children as classless persons—they are all students. Until the integration movement forced race into the national consciousness, state schools were comfortable with segregation, as they are in today's resegregated school system. They are only aware of the poorer classes when they fail or drop out of school. Otherwise, minorities, the poor, and females are shadowy faces performing standardized educational tasks in penal-like, impersonal classrooms. There is an imaginary conception of public schools that treats all children as equals with equal opportunities to achieve academic success. And this ideological effect persists in spite of mountains of evidence to the contrary. If educational systems were really interested in preparing youth for their lives as citizens in a democratic society, they would have to analyze and rethink their own practices and social functions. This is not something that schools have the power to do, since the licensing, funding, and operation of educational systems is a state matter. Schools are condemned to reproduce themselves and the society no matter how harmful such efforts may be for the educational and psychological well-being of children.

But the passive reception of the arbitrary curriculum and practices of state schools is only the tip of the observable iceberg. These structures were conceived in language; they have survived long after they were developed to solve problems in our nation's past. The methods used to regiment and assimilate immigrants from Europe during the nineteenth century are still being used as the twentieth century comes to a close. Class size, which was always a problem, is sneaking up to forty children in a classroom in many areas of the United States. These practices are legitimized by ideological understandings; they are internalized by the word presentations and social structures that fix them in the shared symbolic order of all citizens. Educational practices are seldom seen as historical products, the result of the system's need to reproduce itself. They are seldom related to the Lancastrian schools for pauper boys, or the need to recreate the labor power of the future in a commodity-producing and consuming society. But within all of these deterministic forces, there are rare evidences of free will and an active pursuit of academic knowledge and success. These are exceptions, however, and the silent armies of immigrant and poor children experience schooling as a succession of traumas and failures. The cultural product of schooling is tied to its social functions, attracting support because of the system's demand that children be prepared to assume duties as adults in a grossly unequal society. Students are given some opportunity and an imaginary order emphasizing the "hope" that they will succeed. There is an obvious and unending tension between the words that describe classroom life and its reality. That reality insists upon a complete transformation of the self of students; in many instances, children must give up their culture and language, while in many others, their sex or race are demeaned. The degradation and humiliation of constant passivity and submission lead to a certain type of student and citizen: he is able to take his place in the classroom or workplace without questioning the social relations that exist there.

The Loss of Personal Identities

In the rigid, tradition-bound structures of state schools, certain questions may surface from time to time. Students may ask, "Who am I and what am I doing here?" They may mourn the loss of personal identities or simply become aware of feelings of malaise and alienation. They may fear that they are losing themselves and gaining very little in return. Their relationships to teachers and fellow students may force them to compartmentalize their egos, splitting them into many parts so that they can satisfy the demands and expectations of others. Their inner selves may draw back from the false faces they must present in the classroom. Or these feelings may be repressed and unavailable to them; feelings of anxiety and humiliation may be expressed by a passivity and disinterest in schoolwork. Students may fear what is happening to them because it happens in public; they may want to escape from the learning situation in the same moment that they find themselves wishing to play out the regimented behaviors of the student role. They may want to be like other students, like those who are praised by parents and teachers. But to take on the identity of others means to give up their essential nature and core. They may react aggressively to the depersonalized relations that are part of state schooling, seeking to assert themselves. Yet they must accept the role and demeanor of the student if schools are to properly identify and assimilate them into their administrative and organizational structures. Children from minority and poor families may find it difficult to accept the hidden biases and prejudices characterizing their educational experiences in mass schools. They may give up trying to learn the language and culture of the school, embracing instead attitudes and beliefs of a subculture. They may seek to maintain their identities and desires, even though this assures their classroom failure. They may become trapped in a submissive, subordinate role that clashes with inner self-perceptions and yearnings for freedom and integrity. They have no subjective existence in classrooms, save when they defy or disobey the commands of the pedagogue. Slowly, many students may come to see their student identities as a false front, one that is in conflict with daily reality. Their identity for teachers and fellow students is constantly established in educational discourses while personal identity hardly exists.

Students want to be recognized as individuals, as persons who are separate and apart from other children. They do not want to be seen as part of the group, or as an object that can be spoken about or evaluated. What the youngster seeks, what every human being needs, is not knowledge but recognition. The rejection and isolation in the classroom lead to a negation of the educational goal. Still, students can and do repress and sublimate their worst experiences, preserving themselves and their mental health. The intensity of humiliations and failures is lessened by their detachment from learning experiences. In classrooms, children learn that they are not the persons they thought they were before their schooling began: they are not competent and worthwhile individuals. Now they are someone else, moving away from symbolic exchanges with parents and friends into an arena where desires and sexual symbols are tightly repressed. By becoming a student for his teacher, the child loses his inner self, at least during the school day. His ego must now use imaginary functions to explain this loss of self, but it does so in ahistorical and asocial ways. The unconscious elements in classroom discourses are denied, and consciousness and discipline are emphasized. The imaginary relationship between students and teachers is one of transferred affection and aggressiveness; two egos struggle to make sense of a sociably produced situation. The children become objects who must be moved about and controlled in large groups by their teachers. They are not active doers or subjects in the classroom; rather, they are like workers struggling for recognition and praise, seeking to end chains of signifiers that constantly redefine and demean them. Her decisional rights give the always-talking teacher the role of the competent and knowing person, the boss. Children are thus able to project onto these adults the traits and personalities of significant others with whom they have dealt in the past. The teacher-student relationship is an imaginary and symbolic one; both are busy trying to maintain their senses of self between narcissistic images of personal and institutional lives. But teachers are not the authority figures who lived in their students' pasts. They are actual people, exercising powers of control with the advice and consent of the state. When students refuse to respond to the unconscious and conscious demands of schooling, they stop communicating as objects and assert themselves as subjects, and their identification as school failures begins.

Raising Consciousness

From this discussion, we can see how many might believe that the freedom, choice, and individuality of human life is illusory. Yet a teacher teaching in a ghetto school may develop higher levels of consciousness. She may come to see her students in a more empathetic way, praising their courage and endurance in difficult circumstances. She may blame herself for not being more effective in her inner-city classroom, thinking that if she got to know her children better, they would improve their schoolwork. (Perhaps the ideological understanding of her pedagogic efforts may have blinded her to the structural problems facing teachers and students in state schools.) Later, she may come to see that it is not really her fault that the work is so boring and meaningless, and that she is not to blame for everything occurring in her classroom. She may come to see that it is the class character of schooling in capitalist society that is at the root of her troubles; she may blame the "system" for her inability to adequately instruct minority and poor children. These insights would not preclude her responsibilities in the situation; rather, they might allow her to grasp some of the hidden social and linguistic structures working against her and her students. She may come to realize that how we validate inequalities in American society is unfair and unreasonable. Students are forced to compete, even though their backgrounds, skills, and abilities differ widely. In capitalist society, education has been enmeshed in an ideology of equal opportunity and access, as a legitimate way of designating work roles in our pyramidal social structure. Quite often, teachers and students come to accept this ideology, blaming themselves for educational and social failures.

These ideologies are rooted in the thoughts and traditions of American culture and are accepted by immigrants and others who have come to the United States in the past. Yet such ideas distort the nature of schooling, ignoring the state's interests and concerns with inculcation and the social reproduction of society. They are anchored in the lived experiences of Americans but do not provide a realistic appraisal of past or present conditions. Still, our teacher can explore the conflicts and contradictions taking place in her classroom; she can press for a closer match between stated ideals and classroom realities. She is more than a mere category in the symbolic and social structures of schooling, although she is that as well. Yet even within the deterministic elements of classroom life, she can still react to her situation as an individual. A Freudo-Marxian approach to such problems must be based on materialism and the lived experiences of teachers and students. Of course, the teacher's way of thinking and speaking will be burdened by bourgeois values and thought; they will be expressions of her unconsciousness. Her problems may come from the way she thinks and speaks about students and how she sees her own role in their education. She may come to see that much of her feelings and experiences are caused by her class position and the positions of her students. She may see that there is a basic contradiction between her desire to help children and her acceptance of a position in a state school.

Even so, she can still exercise free will in her classroom, challenging the ways she thinks and feels about herself, her work, and her students. She may come to realize her ineffectiveness because of the practices and curriculum she uses and because of her own biases. She may become more aware of the cramped tenements that students live in and the mean circumstances of their daily lives. Thinking about these things, she may get to know her students' parents; she may learn that their language and culture at home is quite different from the one she demands in her classroom. And she may come to see how unfair it is to educate children in such an unequal competitive ethos. Our teacher may learn that her children are programmed for failure even before they are born, no matter what she does in her classroom; they are not going to Harvard, and they will not get the better jobs when they reach adulthood. Still, this teacher may decide to create a supportive environment in her classroom; she may decide to give all her energies to making the learning experience a liberating one for herself and the children she serves.

This kind of thinking can and does take place now and then, influencing how teachers think about and work with students. Such teachers begin to doubt all the ideas and beliefs that have been handed down to them by their own parents and teachers, coming to see that certain objective conditions of life deeply affect the experiences of all students. Individuals and their society are too intertwined; a teacher's failure or success is the result of both her personal qualities and the social conditions and relationships that children have experienced in their past. As our teacher becomes more aware of the objective structures in her classroom situation, she will also become more aware of how class, race, ethnicity, and sex shape her relationships with students. She will come to see how her life has been limited by class background, determining where she would live, with whom she would associate, the primary language and culture she would learn, and so on. And she may come to see that the lives of students are also formed by these ideological and cultural effects.

To accept a linguistically constructed world alone is to condemn people to a robotized existence, free of hope. It is to deny individuals the consciousness that both psychoanalysis and Marxism believe is man's only hope for conquering his misrecognitions and false consciousness. The causes of school failure can be found in the class positions of students and in the language, culture, and behavior of individual youngsters. Denying a place for free will in the conduct of human affairs denies people the opportunity to improve their conditions or to understand the effects of the unconscious and class conflicts on social relationships.

Our teacher must break her position of detachment and disinterest in the nature and structure of her own personality and in those of students. She must become more conscious of her inner experiences and the ways they affect what is happening to her and the students in her classroom. Conflicts can be discovered and monitored in the mind and in the social arena; impulses and the discourses of class conflict can be identified and understood by the inquiring individual. The struggle between our teacher and her students occurs within a framework of social, political, and economic structures, but it is played out in everyday practice through language, culture, and unconscious communications. It is in practice that our theories of the individual must be constantly reformulated. The struggle to end the inequities in bourgeois society is not only an economic one, but thought and language are supporting such arrangements as well. Families and schools are political and cultural instruments of the bourgeois state, incessantly waging the cultural class struggle. These state apparatuses transmit the ideology of democratic freedom and equality to children who must struggle for recognition and attention in overcrowded, authoritarian, unequal, and underachieving mass schools. When our teacher comes to see the conflict that exists between her own desire to educate and help students and the practices and conditions of her work, her higher level of consciousness will permit her to embark upon new ways of doing the work. If teachers want to help students, they will have to demand educational changes in the number of children they serve each day. But such a politics of education has proved fruitless in the past and may prove so again. Teachers cannot expect real reform until capitalism itself changes radically; they need to begin their struggle for a more child-oriented, more democratic educational system in the schools and communities of America. The inertia they will face is formidable: Americans have become comfortable with detached ways of interacting with one another. They resist efforts to form more meaningful relations or to establish more equality in their competition-obsessed social system.

Nor can we naively continue to hope that socialism will make these problems of human nature disappear. Changes in property relations will not change the aggressive and erotic tendencies of human beings; it will not quiet the restless id nor the unconscious yearnings and communications of the libido. The human needs that are going unmet in American life must be discussed in their present-day contexts, even if a sterile reformism is all we can reasonably hope for. The struggle between capital and labor will not disintegrate, and the social formations that support bourgeois culture will not disappear either. Reformism may allow us to discuss certain relationships in capitalist society on a superficial level, placing blame for social inaction and failure on the shoulders of individuals or organizations. But this approach does not deal with the structural and systemic problems at the heart of alienation in mass society. These deeper structural features of capitalism can provide our teacher with a set of predetermined realities that shape her individual experiences in the classroom. For her to begin to exert her heightened consciousness and free will, she will have to understand them; she will have to unmask and mold them closer to her own wishes and the needs of her students.

Thinking about minority and poor children in inner-city schools, we can begin to see their experiences in more radical terms. These children are not workers or inmates, yet they are apprenticing for their future work in a penal-like setting. The role of minority and poor students in American society is well known: they are condemned to a lesser life and existence because of their failure to master an arbitrary, class-biased pedagogy. But their failures are not only in the realms of education and economics. Culturally, they are condemned to a life of destitution, even as their chances of learning to speak and associate with people from other classes and races are limited by apartheid-like segregation. Inner-city children have an important role to play in the reproductive functions of state schools and society. They reinforce and validate bourgeois ideologies of free and fair competition in public schools; they legitimate the ways that wealth and power are passed from one generation to the next; and they provide capital with a reserve army of labor that holds down the wages of all workers. Within the social relations of classroom life, dominant ideological effects create the symbolic controls and violence that so influence the behavior of youth. Students have little chance of unmasking the imaginary orders of schools and families; they have little chance to see the distortions existing in the ideas and beliefs they learned at their mother's knee. (Parents and teachers possess the power and authority to teach valid forms of knowledge, and these are laden with unintended and hidden consequences.) Students suffer most from how they are taught: social positions place many of them at a disadvantage, distorting their entire educational experiences. This forces them into greater self-consciousness. They look for and find ways of assuaging the pain and humiliation of unpleasant schooling conditions.

Bourgeois ideology is taught, first and foremost, in the bossism and arbitrariness of state pedagogues. It is there that the conditions of an employee society are replicated, inuring students to the worst excesses of their future experiences in the labor market. The valid knowledge of arbitrary state curricula is produced by the social and economic demands of capitalist economics. Teaching and learning take place in tradition-bound classrooms where teachers mimic the unquestioned authority of capitalists. An enlightened education would have to begin with a historical review of the educational system and the development of its present-day practices. Once students (and teachers) are aware of how they are influenced by these methods from the past, they can begin to use their new consciousness to change them. Once they are aware of the unconscious structures and processes used in communications between them, they can begin to make more enlightened choices. Teachers and students can then ask themselves: "Is it possible to educate anyone in these huge state institutions that now monopolize schooling? Can the authoritarian relationships existing in classrooms lead to an inner-directed, inquiry-oriented, moral education?" Unfortunately, these questions may lead many to abandon public schools. The alternative is to maintain the practices of the past, practices that have failed so dismally. Students will not learn much in such schools, but they can read and think about things when they are out of school. Teachers may have to organize themselves into trade unions before they can make themselves heard in state bureaucracies. Perhaps then, both teachers and students can gain insight into their own needs and desires and the social relations of schooling as it now exists. Not new ways of teaching and learning but new and more equal relationships are needed if children are to be prepared for life as literate citizens in a democratic ethos.

When teachers and students become more socially conscious, they have just begun their work together. They must also learn more about the unconscious forces dominating personalities and psychic desires. They must evaluate classroom conditions by asking whether they make sense when social and psychological needs are considered. This may lead to frustration. Both groups may shudder when they perceive how little power they really have over their classroom activities. They may feel revulsion when they learn how capitalism uses their work together to legitimate the continued inequalities of our system.

Possibilities

Let us consider further the relations that could develop between teachers and students if their consciousnesses were raised. We do not presume that relations between them must always be governed by ideological effects and slogans. But it is true that much of their language and culture works against changes of any kind. It is when teachers attempt to change things on their own that they begin to feel the hidden power and authority of those who operate the schools. They find that they must re-evaluate their self-images and the images of others with whom they work, seeking to understand the effects of unconscious impulses and desires. They may have to relive some of their early childhood experiences in schools, remembering how they responded to the arbitrary power and control of adults. Then they will be able to grasp the realities of social power at work in their classrooms, imposing definitions on everything that happens there.

Teachers may come to see that their experiences as youngsters affect how they act in classrooms today. They may realize that opposing the pedagogic practices and symbolic controls of the school may not help children who are trapped there. The bourgeois character of schools is supported by deep, traditional ideologies: the competitiveness, individualism, and egoistic features of learning in state schools persist in spite of the inequities and alienation that characterize schooling in mass society. The functions of bourgeois schools (to prepare youth for life in an impersonal, work-oriented society) has not changed with the new conditions of the late twentieth century. The power that operates state schools is also intrinsic to the language and culture of those who study and work in them; it is not just pressures and ideologies from unseen, outside forces. Teachers, parents, and others transmit the reproduction of the educational and social relations in society without thought or discussion. This is how ideology works in the cultural class struggle: assimilating bourgeois ideas means absorbing the ideologies and imaginary order of the relations of power now in existence.

Communications between teachers and students are distorted by the worker-boss dialectic so characteristic of state schools. If students are apprentice workers, then passive, detached, and obedient responses are good practice for their futures in capitalist workplaces. It is because they live in the symbolic and imaginary order that children accept the arbitrary power of teachers. But their needs and desires place them in perpetual conflict with the conditions of their servitude, even when they are unaware of these unconscious communications. This is the essential feature of the dialectic, a process occurring beneath the surface of life in the variant total institutions we call schools. Children are miniature human beings; they have the moral and psychological need to assert themselves, to differentiate themselves from others, and to regain control over their thoughts and bodily movements. Schooling regiments the child and negates his social and psychological needs and nature, failing to provide discourses that raise his consciousness about lived experiences at home or in school.

Therefore, many children who love the idea of learning and would dearly like to do well in school harbor unpleasant and angry wishes toward teachers. They come to resist the authoritarian practices and personalities that abound in state schools. Children need to become worthwhile and competent persons in the eyes of the significant adults with whom they work. But they cannot realize themselves until they become conscious of their own unconscious desires and memories, and they cannot begin such processes until schooling makes fundamental changes in its relation to them and to the power structures in mass society. The material changes in capitalist systems determine the nature of cultural and class struggles in schools and elsewhere. For teachers and students, there is constant struggle and tension, since the demands of state schools and those of parents and children differ significantly. Students can never accept the conditions of schooling without abandoning their personal selves, without sacrificing their human qualities in the pursuit of a sterile conformance.

Students often learn that their upbringing has much to do with their way of thinking about schools. Their subordinacy reproduces the structure of social relations in the workplace. The smallest changes in how teachers relate to students would have profound consequences for those who control and operate educational systems. These would alter the kind of students who move into the workplace, exacerbating the class struggle and creating greater social discontent than now exists.

One way to effect change in classrooms would be to deny teachers the right to decide things there. With so much dissatisfaction, traditional ways of doing things could be challenged by any of the participants. Teachers could make more demands on administrators, urging them to include more relevant curricula. Board members and others would probably feel threatened by such demands if they disturbed their right to choose texts and evaluate what took place in schools. Such officials know that they have been vested with the power and authority of the state to set policy and hire teachers and administrators, so that the goals of the system can be realized. They may express regret when they see how badly schools are doing, but they probably blame others for such poor showings. How they see the tasks of schooling is very much influenced by legal-rational authority and the thought processes that were ingrained in them many years ago when they were schoolchildren themselves. If teachers were given more power to decide things, administrators and board members would lose some of their power. They might feel diminished by these changes. They might believe that teachers were unfit and unable to see the "big picture"; they could never organize and operate a complex school system efficiently. Board members and administrators might demean the efforts of teachers to change the state's mandated curriculum, pointing out the competitive nature of schooling in the state and nation. On the other hand, they might become angry with the "rebellious teachers," thinking that the schools would be better off without them. They might feel that the teachers were unappreciative of efforts on their behalf. This, in turn, could lead to further conflicts and an open breach between teachers and those with whom they work.

It might be that only after such intense conflicts could teachers become aware of the unconscious forces generating the behavior and confusions within schools. Reformists could begin by seeing children as individuals having their own needs and desires; they might put aside the regimented and meaningless learning experiences of the traditional classroom, seeking greater relevancy in pedagogic efforts. They might come to see the profound ambivalence governing student attitudes and behavior, and they might decide to change their arbitrary actions. The ideas teachers have about children will evolve as they get to know them better. They will come to see themselves differently as well. For a while, they may be troubled and confused by the eruption of negative emotions occurring when students can finally speak their minds. But then they will come to understand how oppressive classroom life has been for their students and for themselves.

These changes in thinking will be difficult. They will be opposed by our own families and friends and a whole host of other good people who find great comfort and peace in the old ways, the old ideologies. Those who wish to search for the truth of their own natures, and in the social relations that exist in capitalist cultures, will experience many moments of confusion and doubt as they struggle to create approximate understandings of the symbolic order within which they live. But the subordination of students and workers has led to an illiterate, nonreading population unable to meet the challenges and dangers of life in the twenty-first century. Searching for higher levels of consciousness can give us an opportunity to gain some control over our own lives and relations with others living and working in capitalist systems.

Notes

Chapter 1

1. Lacan, Jacques. (1989). *Speech and Language in Psychoanalysis.* (Trans. Anthony Wilden). Baltimore and London: Johns Hopkins University Press: 263–68.
2. Ibid., 270.
3. Winnicott, D. W. (1953). "Transitional Objects and Transitional Phenomena." *International Journal of Psychoanalysis, 34:* 89–97.
4. Blanck, Gertrude, and Blanck, Rubin. (1974). *Ego Psychology: Theory and Practice.* New York: Columbia University Press: 210–13.
5. Lacan, Jacques. (1991). *The Seminar of Jacques Lacan.* (Ed. Jacques-Alain Miller; trans. Sylvana Tomaselli). New York: W. W. Norton: 120–21.
6. Levi-Strauss, Claude. (1969). *The Elementary Structures of Kinship.* New York: Beacon Press.
7. Saussure, Ferdinand de. (1965). *Cours de Linguistique Generale.* Paris: Payot: 84–89.
8. Levi-Strauss, Claude. (1969). *The Elementary Structures of Kinship.*
9. Lacan, Jacques. (1989). "Lacan and the Discourse of the Other." In Jacques Lacan, *Speech and Language in Psychoanalysis:* 205–8.
10. Freud, Sigmund. (1989). *The Ego and the Id.* New York: W. W. Norton: 26–32.
11. Lacan, Jacques. (1989). *Speech and Language in Psychoanalysis:* 270–73.
12. Mauss, Marcel. (1966). *Sociologie et Anthropologie.* Paris: PUF: ix–lii.

Chapter 2

1. Mahler, M. S. (1968). *On Human Symbiosis and the Vicissitudes of Individuation.* New York: International Universities Press; see also Mahler, M. S. (1963). "Thoughts About Development and Individuation." *The Psychoanalytic Study of the Child.* New York: International Universities Press: 18; Kris, E. (1951). "The Recovery of Childhood Memories in Psychoanalysis." *The Psychoanalytic Study of the Child;* and the work of H. Hartmann.

2. Lacan, Jacques. (1989). *Speech and Language in Psychoanalysis.* Baltimore and London: Johns Hopkins University Press: 290-91; see also Laing, R. D. (1965). *The Divided Self.* Harmondsworth, England: Pelican Books.

3. Fromm, Erich. (1969). *Marx's Concept of Man.* New York: Frederick Ungar: 169-77.

4. Kojeve, Alexandre. (1969). *Introduction to the Reading of Hegel* (Ed. Allan Bloom; trans. James H. Nichols, Jr.). New York: Basic Books: 552-53.

5. Kojeve, Alexandre. (1989). "Lacan and the Discourse of the Other." In Jacques Lacan, *Speech and Language in Psychoanalysis:* 192-96.

6. Roudinesco, Elisabeth. (1986). *Jacques Lacan & Co. A History of Psychoanalysis in France, 1925-1985.* Chicago: University of Chicago Press: 69-71.

7. Ibid.: 142-44; see also Lacan, Jacques. (1991). *The Seminar of Jacques Lacan Book II.* (Trans. Sylvana Tomaselli). New York: W. W. Norton.

8. Lacan, Jacques. (1989). *Speech and Language in Psychoanalysis:* 184; see also Benton, Ted. (1984). *The Rise and Fall of Structural Marxism.* New York: St. Martin's Press.

9. Levi-Strauss, Claude. (1966). *The Savage Mind.* Chicago: University of Chicago Press; see also Sapir, Edward in Lacan, Jacques. (1989). *Speech and Language in Psychoanalysis.*

10. Rothstein, Stanley W. (1991). *Identity and Ideology: Sociocultural Theories of Schooling.* Westport, Conn.: Greenwood Press: 68-69; see also Benton, Ted. (1984). *The Rise and Fall of Structural Marxism.*

11. Lacan, Jacques. (1989). *Speech and Language in Psychoanalysis.* 262-70; see also Lacan, Jacques. (1991). *The Seminar of Jacques Lacan Book II.:* 115-16, 168-69, 306-7.

12. Freud, Sigmund. (1960). *The Ego and the Id.* (Trans. Joan Riviere). New York: W. W. Norton: 63-66.

13. Freud, Sigmund. (1965). *The Interpretation of Dreams.* (Trans. James Strachey). New York: Avon Books: 283.

14. Laing, R. D. (1960). *The Divided Self.* Harmondsworth, England: Pelican Books: 94-95.

15. Lacan, Jacques. (1989). *Speech and Language in Psychoanalysis:* 264-66.

Chapter 3

1. Freud, Sigmund. (1961). *Civilization and Its Discontents.* (Trans. James Strachey). New York: W. W. Norton: 46-50.
2. Lacan, Jacques. (1989). *Speech and Language in Psychoanalysis.* (Trans. Anthony Wilden). Baltimore and London: Johns Hopkins University Press: 249-51.
3. Benedict, Ruth. (1949). "Continuities and Discontinuities in Cultural Conditioning." In *A Study of Interpersonal Relations* (Ed. Patrick Mullahy). New York: Hermitage Press: 305-6.
4. Radin, Paul. (1953). *The World of Primitive Man.* New York: Henry Schuman: 106, 126, 130.
5. Stein, Maurice. (1960). *The Eclipse of Community.* New York: Harper and Row: 239.
6. Ibid., 241-42.
7. Bendix, Reinhard. (1958). *Max Weber: An Intellectual Portrait.* New York: Doubleday: 215-22.
8. Ibid., 42-42.
9. Ibid., 250-52; see also Lacan, Jacques. (1991). *The Seminar of Jacques Lacan Book II.* (Trans. Sylvana Tomaselli). New York: W. W. Norton: 260-63.
10. Bendix, *Max Weber,* 21-22.
11. Ibid., 29-33.

Chapter 4

1. Braverman, H. (1974). *Labor and Monopoly Capital.* New York: Monthly Review Press: 139-45.
2. Johnson, D. (1981). "Althusser's Fate." In *London Review of Books.* April 16-May 6 Issue: 13-15.
3. Benton, T. (1984). *The Rise and Fall of Structural Marxism.* New York: St. Martin's Press: 99-107.
4. Guess, R. (1981). *The Idea of a Critical Theory.* Cambridge, England: Cambridge University Press: 1-22.
5. Smith, S. (1984). *Reading Althusser: An Essay on Structural Marxism.* Ithaca, N.Y., and London: Cornell University Press: 128-34.
6. Seidler, V. J. (1980). *One Dimensional Marxism.* London and New York: Allison and Busby: 146-49.
7. Bourdieu, P., and Passeron, J. C. (1977). *Reproduction in Education,*

Society and Culture. London and Beverly Hills: Sage Publications: 194–201.

8. Rothstein, S. W. (1991). *Identity and Ideology: Sociocultural Theories of Schooling*. Westport, Conn.: Greenwood Press: 1–9.

9. Sarason, S. (1983). *Schooling in America: Scapegoat and Salvation*. New York: Free Press: 109–11.

10. Bernstein, Basil. (1990). *The Structuring of Pedagogic Discourse*. Vol. IV, *Class, Codes and Control*. London and New York: Routledge: 133–40.

Chapter 5

1. Bernstein, Basil. (1990). *The Structuring of Pedagogic Discourse*. Vol. IV, *Class, Codes and Control*. London and New York: Routledge and Kegan Paul: 45–46, 134–35; see also Bourdieu, Pierre. (1977). *Outline of a Theory of Practice*. (Trans. Richard Nice). Cambridge, England: Cambridge University Press: 190–97.

2. Bourdieu, Pierre. (1976). *Reproduction in Education, Society and Culture*. London and Beverly Hills: Sage Publications: 152–53.

3. Rothstein, Stanley William. (1979). "Orientations: First Impressions in an Urban Junior High School." *Urban Education* 14 (1) (April): 91–116.

4. Alexander, Jeffrey C. (1983). *The Classical Attempt at Theoretical Synthesis: Max Weber*. Berkeley and Los Angeles: University of California Press: 58–60.

Chapter 6

1. Freud, Sigmund. (1977). *Introductory Lectures on Psychoanalysis*. (Ed. and trans. James Strachey). New York: W. W. Norton: 21–22; 295–97.

2. Clarke, S., Seidler, V. J., McDonnell, K., Robins, K., and Lovell, T. (1980). *One Dimensional Marxism: Althusser and the Politics of Culture*. London and New York: Allison and Busby: 204–7.

3. Lacan, Jacques. (1991). *The Seminar of Jacques Lacan: Book II*. (Ed. Jacques-Alain Miller; trans. Sylvana Tomaselli). New York and London: W. W. Norton: 20–21.

4. Waller, Willard. (1932). *The Sociology of Teaching*. New York: Russell and Russell.

Selected Bibliography

Alexander, Jeffrey C. (1983). *The Classical Attempt at Theoretical Synthesis: Max Weber.* Berkeley and Los Angeles: University of California Press.
Bendix, Reinhard. (1958). *Max Weber: An Intellectual Portrait.* New York: Doubleday.
Benedict, Ruth. (1949). "Continuities and Discontinuities in Cultural Conditioning." In Patrick Mullahy (Ed.), *A Study of Interpersonal Relations.* New York: Hermitage Press.
Benton, Ted. (1984). *The Rise and Fall of Structural Marxism.* New York: St. Martin's Press.
Bernstein, B. (1990). *The Structuring of Pedagogic Discourse, Volume IV, Class, Codes and Control.* London and New York: Routledge and Kegan Paul.
Blanck, Gertrude, and Blanck, Rubin. (1974). *Ego Psychology: Theory and Practice.* New York: Columbia University Press.
Bourdieu, Pierre. (1976). *Reproduction in Education, Society and Culture.* London and Beverly Hills: Sage Publications.
Bourdieu, Pierre. (1977). *Outline of a Theory of Practice.* Trans. Richard Nice. Cambridge, England: Cambridge University Press.
Bourdieu, Pierre, and Passeron, J. C. (1977). *Reproduction in Education, Society and Culture.* London and Beverly Hills: Sage Publications.
Braverman, H. (1974). *Labor and Monopoly Capital.* New York: Monthly Review Press.
Clarke, S., Seidler, V. J., McDonnell, K., Robins, K., and Lovell, T. (1980). *One Dimensional Marxism: Althusser and the Politics of Culture.* London and New York: Allison and Busby.

Freud, Sigmund. (1961). *Civilization and Its Discontents.* Trans. James Strachey. New York: W. W. Norton.
Freud, Sigmund. (1965). *The Interpretation of Dreams.* Trans. James Strachey. New York: Avon Books.
Freud, Sigmund. (1977). *Introductory Lectures on Psychoanalysis.* Ed. and trans. James Strachey. New York: W. W. Norton.
Freud, Sigmund. (1989). *The Ego and the Id.* New York: W. W. Norton.
Fromm, Erich. (1969). *Marx's Concept of Man.* New York: Frederick Ungar.
Guess, R. (1981). *The Idea of a Critical Theory.* Cambridge, England: Cambridge University Press.
Johnson, D. (1981). "Althusser's fate." *London Review of Books.* April 16–May 6, 13–15.
Kojeve, Alexandre. (1969). *Introduction to the Reading of Hegel.* Ed. Allan Bloom; trans. James H. Nichols, Jr. New York: Basic Books.
Kris, E. (1951). "The Recovery of Childhood Memories in Psychoanalysis." In *The Psychoanalytic Study of the Child.* New York: International Universities Press.
Lacan, Jacques. (1989). *Speech and Language in Psychoanalysis.* Trans. Anthony Wilden. Baltimore: Johns Hopkins University Press.
Lacan, Jacques. (1991). The Seminar of Jacques Lacan. Ed. Jacques-Alain Miller; trans. Sylvana Tomaselli. New York: W. W. Norton.
Laing, R. D. (1965). *The Divided Self.* Harmondsworth, England: Pelican Books.
Levi-Strauss, Claude. (1969). *The Elementary Structures of Kinship.* New York: Beacon Press.
Levi-Strauss, Claude. (1966). *The Savage Mind.* Chicago: University of Chicago Press.
Mahler, M. S. (1968). *On Human Symbiosis and the Vicissitudes of Individuation.* New York: International Universities Press.
Mahler, M. S. (1963). "Thoughts About Development and Individuation." In *The Psychoanalytic Study of the Child.* New York: International Universities Press.
Radin, Paul. (1953). *The World of Primitive Man.* New York: Henry Schuman.
Rothstein, Stanley W. (1991). *Identity and Ideology: Sociocultural Theories of Schooling.* Westport, Conn.: Greenwood Press.
Rothstein, Stanley William. (1979). "Orientations: First Impressions in an Urban Junior High School." *Urban Education,* 14 (1) (April): 91–116.
Roudinesco, Elisabeth. (1986). *Jacques Lacan & Co. A History of Psychoanalysis in France, 1925–1985.* Chicago: University of Chicago Press.

Sarason, S. (1983). *Schooling in America: Scapegoat and Salvation.* New York: Free Press.
Saussure, Ferdinand de. (1965). *Cours de Linguistique Generale.* Paris: Payot.
Smith, Steven. (1984). *Reading Althusser: An Essay on Structural Marxism.* Ithaca, N.Y., and London: Cornell University Press.
Stein, Maurice. (1960). *The Eclipse of Community.* New York: Harper and Row.
Waller, Willard. (1932). *The Sociology of Teaching.* New York: Russell and Russell.
Winnicott, D. W. (1953). "Transitional Objects and Transitional Phenomena." *International Journal of Psychoanalysis,* 34: 89–97.

Index

Althusser, Louis: and social reproduction, 71–72; and structural Marxism, 141–146

Classroom, and struggle for dominance between teachers and students, 132–139
Class struggle, and human capability, 89–90
Consciousness: and ideology, 156–161; in urban schools, 155
Cultural heritages: and kinship structures, 47–56; and language, 20; and symbolic relationships, 20–23

Descartes, René, and human consciousness, 39

Ego psychologists, and early human interaction, 3

Family relationships: and cultural and moral understandings, 7; and symbolic networks, 7–11
Freud, Sigmund: and collective unconsciousness, 65; and father figure in the law, 60; and fetishism, 148–151; and Marxism, 141–146; and metapsychology, 40–41; and Oedipal period, 16–18; and primitive word presentations, 49

Gramsci, Antonio, and class domination, 71

Hegel, G.W.F.: and self-alienation, 29–31; and self-consciousness, 27–28
Heidegger, Martin, 29
Husserl, Edmund, 29

Identities, personal, and state schools, 153–155
Ideological state apparatuses, and social reproduction, 77–78
Ideology: in action, 72; and cultural effects, 91; defined, 72–77; and family life, 88–89; and practice, 78–79
Imaginary: and the classroom,

117-121; and symbolic order, 25-26, 117
Infancy: first cathexes, 16-20; and neonate's sense of self, 26-27; and sending intentional messages, 9-11
Israelite confederacy: and kinship structures in ancient times, 56-58; and worship of God, 56-57

Kinship structures, and the unconscious, 58-64

Lacan, Jacques: and Henri Wallon, mirror experiments, 34-43; and imaginary and symbolic orders, 118-121; and Marx, 141-146; and the Other, 41-44; and phenomenology, 29; and the "real Other," 3; and unconscious structured as a language, 15-16
Language: and devaluation of student's self-worth, 103-105; and kinship structures, 47-56; and pedagogic work, 93-97; and socialization of the infant, 118-121; and the structure of language, 37-38; and thought, 25-35
Levi-Strauss, Claude: and comparison of cultures and language, 14-15; and Saussure, 39-40; and social reproduction, 64-65

Marx, Karl: and the class struggle, 89-90; and Freud, 141-146; and structural theories, 149-151
Memories, and repression, 41

Normative order: and civil and educational society, 111-115

Oedipal complex, and psychological dimensions of neonate's first identifications, 16-18, 35
Other: and cognition, 35-36; defined, 3-6; and Otherness, 67-68; and pedagogic work, 93-97; in primeval man's first communications, 48; role in communication, 4; and thought, 41-44; and the unconscious, 19-20

Pedagogic action: and historical perspectives on, 151-153; and language, 93-103; and resistances, 106-108; and social knowledge of schools and classrooms, 121-126
Primitive societies, and transition rituals, 54-56
Psychogenetic processes, and sensory perceptions of the world, 25-26

Repression: and the creation of an interpersonal world, 43; and Lacan, 41; and memories, 40-41
Reproduction, social, 64-65; and ideological dominance, 70-71; and labor power, 69-70; and the state, 70
Resistances: and pedagogic action, 106-108; and regression in classroom behaviors, 127

Saussure, Ferdinand de: and acoustic images, 52-53; and the signifier, 38; stages of linguistic development, 14
Schooling: and alienation, 126; and regression, 127
Signifiers, 38

Index

Speech: and class positions of families and individuals, 21–22; and language, 1–3; and linguistic signs, 36–37; and their relationship, 11–13; and the unconscious, 10–11

Structuralists: and the development of language systems, 37; and linguistic meaning, 36–38

Symbolic order: and origins of thought, 40–41; and perceptions of the real world, 60

Thought, and language, 25

Unconscious: and classroom life, 108–110; collective, 64–65; and kinship structures, 58–64; as the Other, 19–20; as a transindividual phenomenon, 18

Urban schools: and business ideology, 83–86; and status quo, 82; and teachers, 82–83

Wallon, Henri: and mirror experiments, 31–34; and schools, 149

Weber, Max, and normative features of civil life and schooling enterprises, 111–115

About the Author

STANLEY WILLIAM ROTHSTEIN is Professor of Education, School of Human Development and Community Services, Graduate Department of Educational Administration, California State University, Fullerton. He is the author of *Identity and Ideology: Sociocultural Theories of Schooling* (Greenwood Press, 1991), *The Power to Punish: A Social Inquiry into Coercion and Control in Urban Schools* (1984), *Leadership Dynamics: Advance Perspectives in School Administration* (1986), and articles for *Urban Education* and other journals.

OHIO UNIVERSITY LIBRARY
Please return this book as soon as you have

J
QI